Fanciful Paper
Projects

FANCIFUL PAPER PROJECTS

CREATING YOUR OWN POSH LITTLE FOLLIES

By Sandra Evertson

Sterling Publishing Co., Inc. New York

A Sterling/Chapelle Book

CREDITS

Chapelle, Ltd.:
   Jo Packham, Sara Toliver, Cindy Stoeckl

A Red Lips 4 Courage Book
   Eileen Cannon Paulin, Rebecca Ittner,
   Catherine Yarnovich Risling, Jayne Cosh

Red Lips 4 Courage Communications, Inc.:
   8502 E. Chapman Ave., 303
   Orange, CA 92869
   (714) 289-0139
   e-mail: rl4courage@redlips4courage.com
   web site: www.redlips4courage.com

Pinnacle Marketing Communications

Library of Congress Cataloging-in-Publication Data

Evertson, Sandra.
   Fanciful paper projects : creating your own posh little follies / Sandra Evertson.
      p. cm.
   "A Sterling/Chapelle Book."
   Includes index.
   ISBN 1-4027-2005-X
   1. Paper work. I. Title.
   TT870.E89 2005
   745.54—dc22

                                                    2004025661

1 0 9 8 7 6

Published in paperback in 2005 by Sterling Publishing Co., Inc.
387 Park Ave. South, New York, NY 10016
©2005 by Sandra Evertson
Distributed in Canada by Sterling Publishing
% Canadian Manda Group, 165 Dufferin Street
Toronto, Ontario, Canada M6K 3H6
Distributed in Great Britain by Chrysalis Books Group PLC,
The Chrysalis Building, Bramley Road, London W10 6SP, England
Distributed in Australia by Capricorn Link (Australia) Pty. Ltd.
P. O. Box 704, Windsor, NSW 2756, Australia

Printed and Bound in China
All Rights Reserved

Sterling ISBN 1-4027-2005-X Hardcover
         ISBN 1-4027-2752-6 Paperback

For information about custom editions, specials sales, premium and
corporate purchases, please contact Sterling Special Sales
Department at 800-805-5489 or specialsales@sterlingpub.com.

FOREWORD

The World is My Oyster

When I was a child, my mother could create just about anything I wanted. I remember once she even made me a giant papier mâché swan with curly crepe paper feathers. From her I learned that anything I could dream up, I could figure out a way to make—and you can too.

I've been a collector ever since I can remember. When I was 4 years old, I would gather pretty stones, fossils, seashells, marbles, bottle caps, cereal prizes, crackerjack toys, and paper dolls. As I grew older, I started saving things with more sentimental attachments—a valentine from my first grade "crush," cute gift wrap from a present given to me by my cousin, Cathy, birthday cards, interesting old photos, fabrics, labels, millinery flowers, bows, buttons, laces. Shall I go on?

Several years ago, while at an antique doll sale, I happened upon a flyer advertising classes for making reproduction porcelain dolls. It sounded great! I talked my mom into going with me and so began a wondrous journey with design influences like Alice in Wonderland, Willie Wonka and characters from "Great Expectations."

In this class, I made some exact reproductions and some art dolls that included a half porcelain doll/half teapot, delicate long-legged ballerinas, and soup can dolls. Each doll had so many different pieces that I would sometimes think, "Yahoo! I found it!" once the perfect missing element was discovered.

A lifelong passion for dreaming up beautiful things has led me to communicate through my art. It makes me so happy to be able to create and live with my work, and I am fortunate that I can share my methods to the madness.

I hope you will have many hours of fun with this book and that you will enjoy making your own Posh Little Follies. Everyone should have a little folly in their lives!

Sandra Evertson

Dedication

Thank you to my multi-talented husband, David—musician, builder, typist, photographer, and my biggest supporter.

To my father and mother, Gerald and Mary, for making me believe that I could do anything I set my mind to and for passing along their many talents; my sister, Melanie, for having a bigger car than mine; my brother, Michael, a sculptor and all-around genius—"Are you in, genius?"

To Judy Criscoe and Gary Beckman for teaching me how to use a copier.

To Lillie Mae Williams for being a lover of antique ephemera too!

And finally, a very special thanks to Eileen, Jo, Rebecca, Cathy, and Lauren for believing in me, this project, my work, and making my dream a reality.

5

TABLE OF CONTENTS

Foreword 5

Introduction 8

Getting Started 10

    Tips & Tricks of the Trade 11

Favorite Sources 13

Violet and Friends 16

Petunia Art Doll 20

Paper Maker's Heart Bandbox 24

Prima Ballerina 28

Theatre La Rousse 32

  Cupcake Papier Mâché Box 38

   Mint Julep 44

  Spodie Odie Doll 52

  Higgins Playing Card Art Doll 58

    Milles Bons Baisers 62

     Flora Fairies—Lolly 70

    Tarts Business Card Art Dolls 76

    Petite Theatre 84

      Babbit's Cabbage 92

      Posies 100

   Tempus Fugit 104

   Pipsqueak 110

    Gibberish Bandbox 118

   The Artist & Her Techniques 123

Acknowledgements 124

Index 126

INTRODUCTION

Several years ago, Sandra Evertson envisioned a fanciful way to make paper theaters, bandboxes, ornaments, and art dolls. The technique was built on her love of ephemera, and her affinity for turn-of-the century papers, textiles, and photographs. These art pieces, small in stature but distinct in character, have become a passion for this artist and her clients, who snap them up faster than she can cut, decoupage, and paste.

In this book, Sandra shares the story behind each piece, which she has affectionately termed Posh Little Follies. Various pieces took weeks, while others took form once she set eyes on a particular photograph. While many of the projects in this book took countless hours to develop, Sandra makes it fun and easy to construct your own in much less time.

Sandra provides step-by-step instructions and the necessary paper elements, which can be photo-copied straight from this book. Some are embellished with everyday items such as pipe cleaners and ribbons, and others are glistening with rhinestones, beads, and glitter. All are made with one key component: fanciful papers.

Following each project description you will find copies of the actual papers Sandra put together for each piece. All you have to do is photocopy the pages in color and follow the instructions. You'll be surprised at just how simple it is to craft your own folly.

You'll also get a little taste of what it's like to be an artist, and experience the creative energy behind each project.

June 1st 1873.

Messrs ...

... will introduce to your honora... ...nfield Success, of this city, who visits ... for the purpose of procuring a situatio... ...anvassing agent, for Hill's Manual ...

...from a... ...nesty, industry, and stead... ...k him such a person ... ...oy, if you need ... ...take great pleasure in ... ...our favor- able acqua...

... Respectfully, ...aniel Cunningham.

Getting Started

Before you head to the copier or start cutting, toss any ideas of perfection out the window. If you make small mistakes, there's no need to worry. These designs are meant to be beautiful, not perfect. As we all should know, beauty is not about perfection; beauty is about perception.

Materials You'll Need

- ¼" hole punch
- 1" circle hole punch
- 19- to 24-gauge wire
- 3-D foam dots
- Card stock
- Corks
- Craft mirrors
- Decorative edge scissors

- Heavy cardboard
- Make-up wedge sponges
- Needle and thread
- Papier mâché boxes and ornaments—these come in various shapes and sizes in either kraft brown or ivory color

- Popsicle sticks
- Scissors
- String
- Toothpicks

Adhesives:
- Hot glue
- Matte decoupage glue
- White glue

Embellishments:
- Feathers
- Glitter
- Millinery flowers
- Vintage junk jewelry

Paint items:
- ½" craft paintbrush
- 1" craft paintbrush
- Black paint pen
- Ivory acrylic paint

Tools:
- Awl
- Hammer
- Nails

- Needle-nose pliers
- Rivets and rivet tool

- Small clamps
- Wire cutters

Now that you have all of your supplies, go and create something wonderful!

10

TIPS & TRICKS OF THE TRADE

These paper designs were created using basic crafting techniques anyone can do. Some minor trimming may be required to fit the particular boxes you use. Just remember: You are creating not only a unique design, but an heirloom art piece that will last generations. Some things to keep in mind on your journey to making your own Posh Little Follies:

Circle faces:

When applying circle faces, cut evenly spaced slits all the way around, then apply a thin layer of decoupage glue to the back of the element, starting at the center and working your way outward and around. Using a Popsicle stick, rub gently to burnish down the edges and smooth out any wrinkles. If you still have a few wrinkles, don't worry; they only add character and charm to your piece, much like us! Craft a stand to paint wooden balls in the projects by cutting a 2" by 2" square out of stiff cardboard, then push a 3" nail with a large flat head through the center of the cardboard. Place ball on point and tap down gently with hammer to hold it in place.

Crepe paper:

When cutting out several crepe paper petals or leaves, a quick way to do this is to fold the paper into 2" increments several times, then place pattern over the paper and cut many at once. For crepe paper ruffles, use a tiny dab of hot glue to seal thread to paper; no knots necessary.

Embellishments:

Don't be afraid to make bows out of raggedy old fabric. Some of the best embellishments are made from torn strips of material. A few extra elements have been provided for many of the projects for you to experiment with.

Hole punch:

Use a hole punch to cut decorative dots for projects throughout this book.

Hot glue:

Always use hot glue sparingly.

Paint pen:

Use a paint pen for stripes on dowels and other elements. They are very easy to work with.

Paper effects:

For an antique look, paint black-and-white copies with instant coffee and dry for one minute in the microwave. To get a fantastic "mottled" effect, mix half water and half household bleach and sprinkle lightly on colored construction paper or crepe paper.

Paper elements:

Study each photograph for placement of elements. Apply a thin layer of decoupage glue to card stock before layering paper elements. To smooth out, dab lightly with make-up wedge sponge. Unless other- wise noted, there's no need to apply a top coat as long as you seal the edges down well. If you like, you can give the piece a light spray with a matte finish sealer.

FAVORITE SOURCES

Sandra Evertson is always on the lookout for the unusual. It could be an old cigar band or remnants of a hat dating back to the Roaring '20s. It may be an object, or the odd color of an item. Sandra looks for things that tell a story, or items that simply appeal to her. These things she finds in shops and stores just as eclectic and personable as the artist herself.

Sandra's Posh Little Follies are the result of a good day at a thrift store, antique mall, or estate sale. That single element—be it a piece of fabric, an old photograph or book, or antique jewelry—ignites her thought process and serves as the basis for one of her art pieces.

Sandra believes that an unusual storefront or façade typically reveals fascinating trinkets for sale once inside. This is why the artist leaves no shop unturned.

Once she has that interesting element in hand, Sandra is off to a crafts store, where she shops for the functional pieces of her designs. In addition to the glue that holds it all together and the embellishments that make it pretty, here she finds the wooden pieces and papier mâché elements that are the base of her designs.

In your own pursuit for the unusual, Sandra suggests:

- Ask friends with similar interests where they shop. You can also ask store owners where other fun shops are located; they are often happy to help out.
- Antique malls are great sources—you have many little shops under one roof.
- Check out ads in local arts-oriented newspapers for great places.
- When looking for materials (elements), think about what something can become, not just what it is. Sometimes a button is not just a button; it could become a hat on a small doll.
- It's a good feeling to take a tattered rhinestone purse and breathe new life into it by using it in a new art piece.
- Keep collecting! You never know when something in your collection will be just right for a piece.
- Read old art and crafting books and magazines for inspiration.
- Keep a sketch book handy so you don't lose a single idea.
- Find your inspiration in everything—a scoop of ice cream, the shape of an old birdcage, the details of a vintage picture frame.
- Don't be afraid to combine seemingly disparate items. The most beautiful forms come from the combination of opposites.
- Be fearless!

Fanciful Paper Projects

VIOLET AND FRIENDS
NARCISSUS AND SECOND PRIZE

This group is certainly mismatched but cozy nonetheless. Really, the only thing they have in common is their size and material. Violet and Narcissus are old tin containers, one a breath freshener, the other a make-up compact. The origin of Second Prize was the State Fair 1902; for what the prize was awarded, the artist is uncertain.

Materials

- Cotton batting
- Hot glue
- Lavender and tan pipe cleaners
- Matte decoupage glue

- Rubber band
- Six 1 ¾" wooden circle disks (2 per doll)
- Small clamps
- String (to make a hanging ornament)

- Tan crepe paper
- Three ⅝" round wooden beads

Optional: Gold and silver pipe cleaners, rhinestones, millinery flowers, ribbon

Instructions

Note: All three dolls are created the same way.

1. Cut out Art Doll Face with pattern (Page 19).

2. Cut slits all the way around (A) and decoupage onto bead. Be sure hole on bead is vertical.

(A)   (B)   (C)   (D)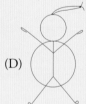

3. Cut five 3" lengths of pipe cleaner. Feed bead through one end. Here you can do an extra step to hang it by making a small hook at top (B).

4. Fold pipe cleaner over string. Put a dab of white glue and pull pipe cleaner and string into bead a bit (C). Lay wooden circle disk flat. Hot glue in place arms, legs, and body pipe cleaners (D). Fold ends of arms and legs over about ¼" to make hands and feet.

16

OPPOSITE: While they may not have much in common, these three are nevertheless best of friends.

5. Add a bit more hot glue and place second disk over this, using clamps to hold together until set.

6. Cut out front and back elements (Page 19); decoupage in place.

To make hair:

Violet: Glue a small wad of cotton batting on head with white glue.

Narcissus: Take a 1" strip of crepe paper, fray on both sides, then white glue in place (E).

(E)

Second Prize: Cut a rubber band into six 1" strips, then white glue onto head (F).

(F)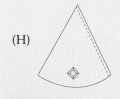

To finish dolls:

1. Cut out crown and necktie (Page 19); decoupage to card stock then hot glue in place. If you prefer, you can make your own crown with pipe cleaners (G).

(G)

2. Glue on embellishments.

3. To construct Burlap Paper Cone Hat (Page 19), cut out then decoupage onto card stock. Cut out hat embellishment (Page 19), then glue on. Hot glue edges together; glue to head (H).

(H)

18

COLGAN'S
VIOLET
CHIPS
THE GUM THAT'S ROUND

Violet

Narcissus

Second
Prize

Second
Prize

"CHIC" HELPS AND HINTS

Compliments of
CHICHESTER
CHEMICAL COMPANY,
Philadelphia, PA.
U.S.A.

Cut
out &
use
for
all...

Face
Pattern

PETUNIA ART DOLL

One rainy afternoon, while shopping in different vintage stores, Sandra found a poem and a family portrait. The poem, written to a beloved mother, served as inspiration for the artist's own Mother Nature, named Petunia. A face on the photograph found that day is the face of Petunia. Sandra has always loved old photographs; she looks at them and wonders who the people were and what their lives were like. She is particularly charmed by the serene expressions on their lovely faces.

Materials

- ¼" hole punch
- 1" circle punch (for face)
- 1" craft paintbrush
- 1 ¼" wooden ball
- Beige crepe paper
- Card stock
- Hot glue
- Matte decoupage glue
- Old millinery flowers
- Popsicle stick
- Silk flower green end cap
- Taupe acrylic paint
- Three pipe cleaners (1 green, 2 tan)
- White glue
- Wooden toothpick

Instructions

1. Paint wooden ball taupe; set aside to dry.

2. Cut out Cone Body paper element (Page 23) and decoupage to card stock; set aside to dry.

3. Cut out armholes with ¼" hole punch.

4. When Cone Body is dry, run a bead of hot glue along top of short edge; glue Cone Body together.

5. Decoupage Bird paper element (Page 22) to card stock; set aside to dry, then cut out.

6. Cut out Face Pattern (Page 23). Place pattern over Mother's Face (Page 23), then cut out.

7. Cut tiny slits all the way around face.

OPPOSITE: Paper flower petals are pieced together to craft the hat and dress on this doll, Petunia, which the artist has nicknamed Mother Nature.

8. Apply thin coat of decoupage on back of face and, starting in the center and working outward, glue face onto wooden ball using the Popsicle stick to lightly smooth out any wrinkles.

9. Use hot glue to attach head to Cone Body.

10. Twist two pipe cleaners (1 green, 1 tan) together; stick through the holes in the body to create arms. (Arms are actually the two twisted pipe cleaners.)

11. From inside cone, add a few drops of hot glue at armholes to stabilize arms. Set aside to dry, then curl end of pipe cleaners to form hands.

12. Cut about 25 flower petals out of crepe paper (use Petal Pattern on Page 23). To expedite this, fold crepe paper into 2" sections several times; place Petal Pattern on top, then cut out.

13. Roll each petal around toothpick. Loosen a bit when you get to flat edge to release toothpick and slide it out, leaving petal curled in tight roll while you do all the rest. (This helps set the curl.)

14. Starting at the bottom of Cone Body front, unroll petal, dabbing white glue only at the base of petal. Attach each to body, working your way around, leaving sections of book print visible.

15. Glue 6-7 petals on top of head to form hat.

16. Glue large Flower paper element (Page 23) to card stock, cut out, then glue onto collar. You may choose to use a silk flower instead.

17. Finish petal hat by gluing silk flower green end cap to top.

18. Glue Bird paper element (above) to second tan pipe cleaner and attach to hand.

Trace over one of the above faces.

Petal Pattern

Face Pattern

HERE'S TO THE PRETTIEST,
HERE'S TO THE WITTIEST,
HERE'S TO THE TRUEST
OF ALL WHO ARE TRUE.
HERE'S TO THE SWEETEST ONE,
HERE'S TO THEM ALL
IN ONE —
HERE'S TO YOU.

A nice sentiment to tuck inside the cone!

PAPER MAKER'S HEART BANDBOX

Among all the things Sandra collects, her most cherished are antique books. Throughout her home, there are shelves full of them. And what hasn't found room on a shelf is stacked in a corner. The beautiful scroll pattern on top of this bandbox came from a Peterson's magazine circa 1869 found in a favorite antique shop called Cleaveland's Antiques in upstate New York. The little curlicues on the letters were the inspiration for this piece.

Materials

- 1" craft paintbrush
- 2 ½" by 4 ½" heart-shaped kraft box (ivory, if available)
- Decorative edge scissors
- Ivory acrylic paint
- Matte decoupage glue

Optional: 1" circle punch

Instructions

1. Paint entire heart box with ivory paint.

2. Cut out Heart-Shaped paper element (Page 27) and decoupage to top of lid.

3. Cut out two ⁵⁄₁₆"-wide strips from Book Page paper elements (Page 26) for lid's edge. Make sure to utilize "key" portions of vintage papers. For example, we used the words Paper Makers and centered the strip on the edge. Decoupage these in place, starting at bottom point of lid.

4. Cut out Striped paper elements (Pages 26, 27) with decorative edge scissors along top edge only. If any trimming needs to be done, trim along bottom. Glue in place along base of box.

5. Cut out Black Dots (Pages 26, 27). You can use 1" circle punch instead of scissors. Decoupage in random places onto base of box.

6. For a nice effect, cut a dot in half and decoupage each half along the bottom edge.

Note: You may choose to seal your finished piece with a coat of decoupage glue.

OPPOSITE: There is pure joy in the freedom of creating. This fancy bandbox to store your secrets in provides a flight of fancy for the creative at heart.

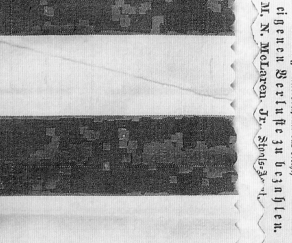

Pretty Buttons Too!

PRIMA BALLERINA

Sandra loves going to the ballet. The music, movement, beautiful costumes—everything about it is romantic and inspiring. What could be more wonderful than sharing in an evening of entertainment fit for a queen? This piece came together one night after attending a Ballet Austin perform-ance of "Hamlet." Sandra came home and gathered papers that brought to mind the scenes still dancing in her head. The few roses seen here are a reminder of the ones tossed on stage for the Prima Ballerina to gather.

Materials

- ¼" hole punch
- 1" craft paintbrush
- 11" by 17" card stock
- 24-gauge wire
- Matte decoupage glue
- Pink glitter
- Three small feathers
- Two pipe cleaners (1 red, 1 tan)
- Wire cutters

Instructions

1. Cut out Body Pieces paper elements (Page 31) exactly and decoupage onto card stock; set aside to dry.

2. Cut out all other paper elements (Pages 30, 31) exactly. Use hole punch to make small black dots.

3. Decoupage elements in place. A few extra elements have been included for you to customize your art doll.

4. When dry, cut out entire piece.

5. Make two wire hoops and glue to back of hands (see diagram below).

6. Twist pipe cleaners together and curl into "horse shoe" shape; hook to ballerina.

7. Embellish dress and shoes with glitter and feathers.

OPPOSITE: The gentle rhythms and sophisticated costumes of a grand ballet have inspired the dance of Prima Ballerina.

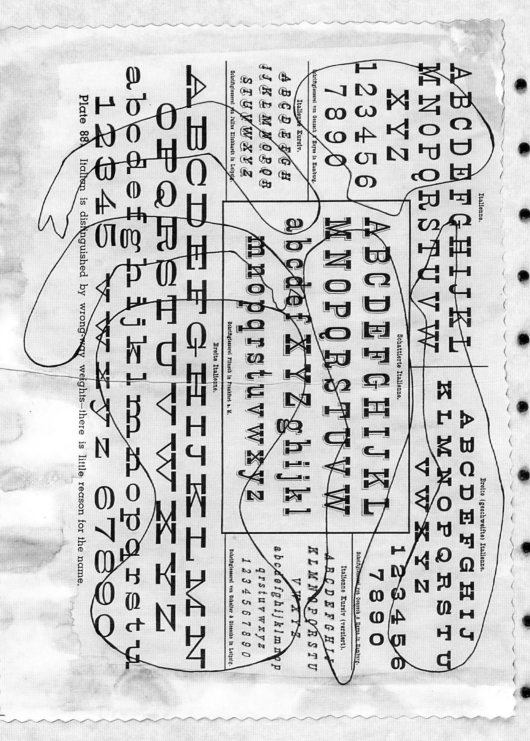

Plate 88. Italien is distinguished by wrong-way weights—there is little reason for the name.

Theatre La Rousse

Pierrot is a 1700s term for a stock comic character in French pantomime, distinguished by a whitened face and wearing loose-fitting clothes. Rousse is French for russet, or reddish. La Rousse was cut from a very old book Sandra found while vacationing in Paris. It contained Aesop's Fables and other stories. The two were a perfect match.

Materials

- 1 ½" by 3" kraft box
- 1 clear 6 mm glass bead
- 1 colored 4 mm glass bead
- 1" by 2" craft mirror

- 1" craft paintbrush
- 19-gauge wire
- Exacto knife
- Hot Glue
- Jewelry finding

- Matte decoupage glue
- Needle-nose pliers
- Wire cutters

Instructions

Note: Some minor trimming may be required to fit your particular box.

1. Center top of lid on Scroll paper element (Page 36). Trace around it, cut out, then decoupage on.

2. Cut out two ½" Book Print paper element strips (Page 37) and glue end to end, around lid sides.

3. Cut out the two Black-and-White paper element strips (Page 36), and do the same. (Be sure to follow "cane" pattern.)

4. Cut out La Rousse–Paris paper strip (Page 35) and glue to one side of box lid.

5. Cut out all other paper elements (Pages 35-37). Glue Alphabet paper element (Page 35) to outside back, Book Print paper element (Page 35) to inside back, two of the 1" Book Print strips (Page 37) to exterior sides and the other two to the interior sides.

6. Glue Valance Scroll and Pierrot (Page 35) to card stock; let dry, then cut out.

7. Glue on Pierrot and Valance paper element backings (Pages 35, 37). Set aside to dry, then cut out. This extra little step will produce a lovely view as you peer into your new treasure and see the reflection!

OPPOSITE: This tongue-in-cheek "objet d' art" is an amusing little trinket and would look great as a hanging decoration.

8. Cut out Mirror Frame paper element (Page 35); decoupage to card stock, let dry, then cut out.

9. Use Exacto knife to cut out center of frame and hot glue to mirror; let dry, then hot glue to "back wall" of box.

10. Glue on tiny Billboard paper element (Page 36) to interior side at an angle.

11. To create a miniature chandelier, cut a 2" piece of wire. Bend a curl on one end with needle-nose pliers; slip on the clear glass bead, poke a hole in center top of box and put straight end of wire through. Slide on jewelry finding and colored bead and curl wire end to close. Either hang piece or display it on its lid as shown here.

12. Glue Pierrot in place, level with bottom edge, then glue the Checkerboard Floor (Page 37) over Pierrot's tab.

13. Glue Valance to ceiling, level with top edge.

Valance Backing

TAB

Valance Scroll

TAB

LAROUSSE - PARIS (VIᵉ)

standen mit den Ärzten un
er Grants, dem Prediger New

er im ganzen Lande, im Süde
der einst den Süden in gewal
e Union vor dem Verfall be
nden Moment zwischen beide
ann von nationaler Bedeutun
wiedergeeinten Nation ange
usammengehörigkeit entspräche
e im ganzen Lande stattfander

des Helden,
us allen Landestheilen am
ging. Die Leiche war unte
Abordnungen von Vereine
Albany gebracht und im do
führte ein besonderer Trauer
und Abordnungen der ver
n hatten, die Leiche nach New
Gelegenheit in eine großartig
usgestellt wurde. Dort sin
00 Männer und Frauen alle
gen, um einen letzten Blick a
fen.
eleitete am 8. August den vor
chenwagen nach dem im Nor
n Hudsonufer herrlich gelege
Gruft für die Aufnahme de
henparade, in der neben de
isationen, Abordnungen be
w. vertreten waren, wurd
arge folgten der Präsident un
aligen Präsidenten Hayes un
toren, Abgeordnete und Ab
r Anzahl. Unter den zwöl

Tochter und mehrere Enkel un
ährigen Freunde und Seelsorg
Sterbelager.
ß und aufrichtig war die Traue
orden. Der Tod des Helden,
gen bezwungen und dadurch di
te, wurde zu einem versöhne
len. Man fühlte, daß ein M
ei, ein Mann, der der ganzen
esem Gefühl der nationalen-Z
die Trauerkundgebungen, di
or allen Dingen auch

das Leichenbegräbniß
beispielloser Betheiligung a
er Stadt New York vor sich
e von Bundesmilitär und vor
Unionskämpfer zunächst nach
ol aufgebahrt worden. Dann
r Gouverneur von New York
Körperschaften sich angeschloss
e im Rathhause, das für diese
e war umgewandelt worden,
7. August wohl an 400,00
der Leiche Grants vorübergez
Züge des Verblichenen zu wer
nübersehbarer Leichenkonduft g
warzen Pferden gezogenen Lei
w York unmittelbar am linke
de Park, wo eine provisorische
ichtet worden war. Die Lei
Arme zahlreiche Milizorgan
my of the Republic u. s.
l Hancock befehligt. Dem S
r seines Kabinets, die ehem
meisten Gouverneure, Seno
von Korporationen in große

Lid

Viehfürsten

rdenbesitzer und Viehzüchter
toritorien unermeßliche Landstre
rn die kleinen Ansiedler, die
a wollen, sich dort niederzul
eß erlassenen Gesetzes hat der
lich errichteten Umzäunungen
ie großen Herdenbesitzer, die im
und der Besiedlung des in
Oklahomagebiets durch weiß
en Weg legten, haben ihr Vie
Zäune entfernen müssen.

Indianerkrieg

e nicht abgegangen. Eine Ap
r Bewachung des dort station
hrem Häuptling Geronimo —
t und Grausamkeit sich bemerk
en Wohnstätten und überfi
rdthaten bezeichneten ihren N
elang es wohl, die Bande zu
inzufangen. Viele derselber
men. Geronimo selbst soll al
m Indianer Territorium ent
orthin geschafften Cheyennen.
hr energische Maßregeln und
en Indianern die Lust zum
h des Präsidenten begab f
und Stelle und sorgte dafü
dianer sich mit Recht beklagte
nd, dessen Schauplatz das
rsichtsmaßregeln in unseren nc
och blieb dort auf unserer

---

n Verwickelung

n den fortwährenden Revolu
anischen Republiken herrschen
Columbia ergriffen worden.
im Staate Panama die Ober
Stadt Panama in Asche. Das
dort wohnenden amerikanischer
r die Landenge von Panama
adung mit der Westküste von
en Umständen erhielt der in der
Jouett von unserer Regierung
z zu diesem Zweck ansehnliche
hickt wurden, setzte nun seine
hn und ihre Endpunkte und
r her. Als später die recht=
ma ergriffen und die Rädels=
en, wurden die amerikanischen

e amerikanische Volk versetzt

Grant,

eneral litt seit längerer Zeit
ur als eine rein örtliche Ent=
hens angesehene Uebel hatt
jahr der Tod des berühmten
n. Damals erholte sich der
te ihn, als die heiße Jahres=
York nicht rathsam erscheinen
rtes Saratoga sehr hoch und
haffen, wo ein persönlicher
Kranken und seiner Familie
. Schon die Fahrt dorthin
, daß man sich keiner Täu=
soweit menschliches Ermessen
dliche Mount McGregor nur
alte Held trug die schweren

---

nehmen, könn
Schulmeister f
rei Quadratm
hrlichen Man

Diese krä
nachen. Der
Nucker haben
oundern. M
lle Leute so r
ichtslauferei n

Diese Ho
mschwung he
ieder das A
förster!" sagte
u quälen und
eschäft hat, d
nd ich sage Ih
inder sind. C
Da sagt mir n
händlicherweis
it ihm auf de
eien über den
B., unser He
uchen.' Das
er weiß, ob i
ufgenommen.
eschichte nicht

„Ja, ja,
nd steckten sic
feifen wieder
nd kannegieß

Mir abe
eschaut hatte,
berall die, di
ffenbarten —
onnen wir die

---

es sei so, u
der edelste
ande, wenn
wäre, — u. j
gewaltigen
nd sprach: „
Ich muß n
aber ich beh
o viel Aerge
lers."
s hatte offe
mann nahn
rtout recht
t und Juden
enn man so
Das glaube
t, was purem
auch eine a
r, den hatte
gebracht, un
, er soll Gif
still: „Mein
Feinde, segne
e Knochen ge
wegen hat d
ssen. Ich
aben."
' applaudiert
Edelmuth, C
ne andere U
Lebensversich
s zum Fens
D, dachte ic
n, so ein ge
en müßten.
uß man davo

Pierrot Backing

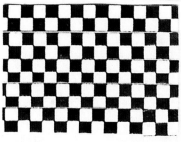

Floor

CUPCAKE PAPIER MÂCHÉ BOX

Sometimes the best ideas come when you least expect them. This curious little fellow came to Sandra one night in a dream. She had just watched "Willie Wonka and the Chocolate Factory" with her niece, Erica, and there he was while she slept, just dancing around without a care in the world. As she keeps an "emergency" sketchbook in her nightstand, Sandra awoke and set about putting the piece on paper. In the morning she gathered what she had envisioned, and voilá!

Materials

- 1" craft paintbrush
- 2 ½" round papier mâché ornament
- 4 ¼" round by 2 ½" high kraft box (ivory, if available)
- 42" beige crepe paper (can use streamer rolls)

- Black acrylic paint
- Card stock
- Copper glitter
- Decorative edge scissors
- Hot glue
- Ivory acrylic paint

- Matte decoupage glue
- Needle and beige thread
- Silver glitter
- Taupe pom-pom
- Wine cork
- *Optional: Silver pipe cleaner*

Instructions

1. Cut wine cork into ½" piece; hot glue to papier mâché ornament.

2. Paint ornament black; set aside to dry.

3. If needed, paint box ivory; set aside to dry.

4. Place box lid on Book Print paper element (Page 41); trace around it, cut out, then decoupage to top of lid.

5. Cut out Side Trim paper elements (Page 42) for the lid, one side straight edge, and one side decorative edge. Start at center back and decoupage on.

OPPOSITE: Written on a small piece of rolled-up paper and tucked inside the Cupcake box is the sentiment: "Good fortune to you. Mine was a beautiful life. Paris Flea Market Designs, Sandra Evertson."

6. Cut two 2 ½"-wide checkerboard band strips (Page 43) for side of box. You will need about 14" to go all the way around. Piece these together to make one long strip, then decoupage onto box. Again, start at center back and go around.

7. Cut out all other paper elements (Page 42).

8. Cut out and decoupage Cone Hat and Stars to card stock; set aside to dry, then cut out.

9. Cut tiny slits all the way around Face paper element (Page 42). Glue in place, smoothing edges down with Popsicle stick (refer to tips on page 11 for techniques).

10. Hot glue head at "cork neck" to center of box top.

11. Cut 42" strip of beige crepe paper about 1" wide with decorative edge scissors on one edge only.

12. With needle and thread, take a running stitch about ½" wide, using ¼" stitches (this can be done, just handle your paper gently).

13. Pull together; hot glue end of thread to crepe paper to seal it.

14. Hot glue ruffle around neck. (You can also just run a bead of hot glue and scrunch up all the way around if you prefer.)

15. Glue four large Star paper elements (Page 42) on ruffle.

16. Hot glue Cone Hat (Page 42) together; hot glue in desired position on head.

17. Glue on Stars, Pom-Pom, and Paper Tinsel or silver pipe cleaner.

18. Embellish Stars with extra glitter.

Und wieget Sorg' und Stra[f]'

Und spricht der Menschheit tröstr[eich]

Hinweg nun Mißgeschick und Beschr[...]

„Und Friede auf Erd[en]"

Da zieht mich's hinunter mit Macht,

Mich mit Menschen zu frei'n

In aller Gassen heiligen Nacht;

Und festlicher Glanz durch alle

In niedrigsten Haus durch des

Seh' ich die Lichter des Chri[st]

Mint Julep

As you can see, the artist loves color! Sandra created this "stars" paper with a box of antique grade school award stars quite by accident. Sheets of delicate ice cream-colored tissue paper were lying on her work table, destined for something entirely different, when she dropped a whole box of the stars on it. The colors were so great together that Sandra ran to her copier once she had everything in place.

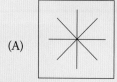

Materials

- ¼" hole punch
- 1" circle punch
- 19-gauge wire
- 3" by 3" square craft mirror

- 4 ½" by 4 ½" by 2 ½" kraft box (ivory, if available)
- Card stock
- Decorative scissors
- Exacto knife

- Hot glue
- Ivory acrylic paint
- Matte decoupage glue
- Small needle-nose pliers
- Wire cutters

Instructions

Note: Copy pink paper with gold stars and polka dots paper twice. If needed, paint box ivory.

1. Cut out two 4 ½" by 4 ½" squares from Pink Star Paper (Page 50).

2. Cut out Numbers Puzzle paper element (Page 47) at 4 ½" by 4 ½".

3. Decoupage one Pink Star Paper to box top exterior, then Numbers Puzzle to box top interior.

4. Cut miniature Crush On You Collages (Page 48) into one long ½" by 18" checkerboard strip. Do this by simply cutting the checkerboard vertically down either side of mirror in each collage. At this point you should have eight 3 ½" pieces. Glue them together end to end. Cut one edge with decorative scissors, then decoupage to top of box lid.

5. With Exacto knife, cut four slits through top of box, stopping 1" from box edge (A).

(A)

OPPOSITE: The delirious little Acrobats were just the bit of humor this piece needed.

6. With needle-nose pliers, gently curl out points to get exploding effect (B).

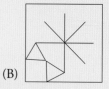
(B)

7. Cut one 4 ½" by 4 ½" square of Polka Dot paper (Page 49), then decoupage onto exterior back of box (what would normally be the bottom).

8. Cut four 2 ½" by 4 ½" pieces of Polka Dot paper for exterior sides of box; decoupage on.

9. Cut four 2 ½" by 4 ½" pieces of Pink Star paper (Page 50) for interior box sides; decoupage on.

10. Decoupage a second 4 ½" by 4 ½" Pink Star paper square (Page 50) to card stock; set aside to dry. Center Interior Star Pattern (Page 47) on Pink Star paper with one point facing straight up. Trace around it with pencil, then cut out (see diagram at right).

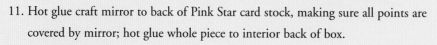

11. Hot glue craft mirror to back of Pink Star card stock, making sure all points are covered by mirror; hot glue whole piece to interior back of box.

12. Cut out all other paper elements.

13. Glue three Pink-and-Black Striped Balls (Page 47) to exterior of box sides.

14. Decoupage Black-and-White Striped Balls, Gray Ball, Pink Gold Star Ball, three Book Print Balls, ¼" Book Print Dot and two Acrobats (Pages 47, 48) to card stock; set aside to dry, then cut out.

15. Glue one Black-and-White Striped Ball and Gray Ball to top of box, making sure to position them half on and half off box.

16. Decoupage back of small Acrobat with Book Print (Page 48).

17. Cut 2" piece of wire; make ¼" loop at one end and ⅛" loop at the other end. Bend ¼" loop horizontally to make a "stand" (see diagram at right).

18. Hot glue small Acrobat to straight end of wire, then hot glue loop stand, with Acrobat, in place on interior of box and cover wire loop with Pink Gold Star Ball (Page 48).

19. Cover exposed glue and wire on back of Acrobat with ¼" Book Print Dot (Page 47).

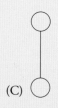
(C)

20. Cut 8 ½" piece of wire; make ½" loops at both ends (C).

21. Put dab of hot glue on #6 square on interior lid of box. Place wire loop here and put 1" book print "Wire Cover Dot" (Page 48) over it; hold in place until dry.

22. Run wire through exploding hole. After about 2", bend wire horizontally (D). Put dab of hot glue on back of large Acrobat (Page 47), cover with book print "Wire Cover Dot"; hold until dry.

23. Hot glue last Black-and-White Ball to end loop using last 1" Book Print "Wire Cover Dot" here.

24. Cut "T" slits in yellow ruffles (Page 47), then glue around neck and ankles.

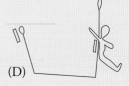
(D)

Interior
Star
Pattern

Wire Cover
Dot

		N.			
6	5	4	3	2	1
7	8	9	10	11	12
18	17	16	15	14	13
19	20	21	22	23	24
30	29	28	27	26	25
31	32	33	34	35	36

V.

O.

S.

ung the... work of Poe... work which wa... number of Poe... cially the ear... sible to o...

...d had some... shed under his... ks, poetry and... s, were always... there was, a...

...ich... wishy-washy... erged rocks of t... rehearse that st... of Poe's writ... volume...

Wire Cover
Dots

...rsa... the... to the west... River route... ...d their successors had traveled, and to blaze a tr... ...us Indians,[1] an overland trail, the trail up the... ...hich the entire emigration was to move. He was... ...homas Fitzpatrick when they made such a trail p... ...ass, the one opening through which wagons could... ...oor to Oregon and California, the true Northwe... ...the party of four who paddled round Great Sal... ...ver the old myth of the River Buenaventura whi... ...lt water westward to San Francisco Bay—though... ...lieve it... But the... are...

ARITHMETICAL PUZZLES.

TROUBLE-WIT.—Take a sheet of stiff paper, fold it down the middle of the sheet, longways; then turn down the edge of each fold outward, the breadth of a penny; measure it as it is folded, into three equal parts, with compasses, which make six divisions in the sheet; let each third part be turned outward, and the other, of course, will fall right; then pinch it a quarter of an inch deep, in plaits, like a ruff, so that, when the paper lies pinched in its form, it is in the fashion represented by A; when closed together, it will be like B; unclose it again, shuffle it with each hand,

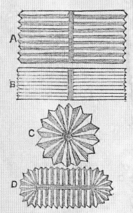

and it will resemble the shuffling of a pack of cards; close it, and turn each corner inward with your fore-finger and thumb, it will appear as a rosette for a lady's shoe, as C; stretch it forth, and it will resemble a cover for an Italian couch, as D; let go your fore-finger at the lower end, and it will resemble a wicket, as E; close it again, and pinch it at the bottom, spreading the top, and it will represent a fan, as F; pinch it half-way, and open the top, and it will appear in the form shown by G; hold it in that form, and with the thumb of your left hand turn out the next fold, and it will be as H.

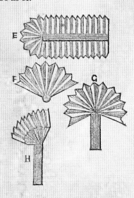

ART RECREATIONS.

J. E. TILTON & Co., 161 Washington street, Boston, publish, for Grecian and Antique Painting, the following elegant Pictures, which we send, post-paid, to any address, on receipt of price. New Pictures constantly being published. Each are prepared on suitable paper, with tints, &c.; and full directions to paint, to mix each color, frame, &c., without extra charge. There are no other publishers of such pictures, nor can any other pictures be made to so fully resemble a canvas oil painting, or remain perfect as these.

The coarse and cheap pictures are not s⸾ people of taste with these beautiful ar⸾

	bes
On the Prairie, very fine,	-
Mary Dow, companion to Barefoot Boy	
The Barefoot Boy, companion to Mary D⸾	
The Rector's Ward,	-
The Marriage of John Alden, in the "C⸾ ship of Miles Standish,"	-
The Virgin and Child, the celebrated ⸾ donna della Scala, by Correggio,	-
Evangeline, from Longfellow,	-
Beatrice Cenci, from the celebrated pain⸾ by Guido,	-
Jean D'Arc,	-
Age and Infancy, a beautiful Family Gr⸾	
The Happy Family, do. do.	
Hiawatha's Wooing, from Longfellow,	
The Farm Yard, by Herring, companion t⸾ Hiawatha's Wooing,	
The Jews-Harp Lesson, by Brunet,	-
The Little Bird, by Brunet,	-
Les Orphelines, copy from celebrated pain⸾ ing,	-

They are the originators of the severa⸾ styles of painting, and publishers of the RECREATIONS. The careful experience ⸾ given in this book, with that of Professo⸾ teacher, who has successfully taught in best seminaries in New England.

Its value to teachers will be obvious, ⸾ at a great distance, for it gives instructi⸾ all materials used, valuable receipts, branches taught are

Pencil Drawing, Oil Painting, Crayon Dr⸾ ing, Paper Flowers, Moss-Work, Papier ⸾ Feather Flowers, Hair-Work, Potichoman⸾ Theorem Painting, Gilding and Bronzing⸾ the Art of Preserving Birds, Grecian P⸾ Painting, Oriental Painting, Wax Flowe⸾ wax, to the beautiful and perfect flowe⸾ Painting, Shell Work, Painting on Grou⸾ Lantern, Imitation of Pearl, Sealing-W⸾ rama Painting, Embroidery, Coloring Pho⸾ Coloring, the Aquarium, &c., &c.

The work is elegantly illustrated, la⸾ $1,50. This and all our pictures and book⸾ by mail.

TABLE RECEIPT⸾

Roly-Poly Pudding.—Make a rich pud⸾ flour and butter, without suet, but as ⸾ Roll it out thin, and cut it to the brea⸾ inches, making it at the same time as lon⸾ but half pound of flour and five ounces of⸾ with water, will probably be sufficient⸾ quite smooth; then spread upon it a thi⸾ berry, currant, or any other sort of jam, but⸾ inch of all the edges bare. That done,⸾ roll of paste will secure the fruit, and th⸾ twisted together for the same purpose. Wr⸾ floured cloth, and boil it for two to thre⸾ to size. Take it up quite hot, and when se⸾ wise. It may appear homely, but it is a⸾ much-admired pudding.

Sponge Cake.—Half pound of Brown ⸾ flour, quarter or half pound of butter, and ⸾ of baking powder, to be very well mixe⸾ three eggs, and beat the yolks and white⸾ fifteen minutes, then add to them quarte⸾ white sugar; mix all together, flavor to t⸾ fifteen minutes; put it into a well-buttered ⸾ round two inches deeper than the tin, and ⸾ oven for one hour.

Spodie Odie Doll

Sandra found a 1920s high school diploma and was
absolutely amazed at the extraordinary artwork on it. She
immediately knew it would make an intriguing object. She
thought, what better to go with a diploma than a class
clown? It wasn't long before she set about making her own
version. This irreverent character is a quaint reminder of
someone we all once knew.

Materials

- 1 ¼" wooden ball
- ½" paintbrush
- Awl (or 3" nail)
- Ball stand (see page 11)
- Beige crepe paper

- Card stock
- Hot glue
- Matte decoupage glue
- Needle and beige thread
- Taupe acrylic paint

- White glue
- Wire cutters
- Wire hanger (need 15" length)

Optional: 1" circle punch, small Pom-Poms

Instructions

1. Copy Orange/Mint Strips (Page 56) paper twice.

2. Place ball on stand.

3. Paint wooden ball taupe; set aside to dry.

4. Decoupage Cone paper element (Page 55) and Hands paper element (Page 57) onto card stock; set aside to dry, then cut out. Note: Use decorative edge scissors along curved bottom edge of cone.

5. Hot glue Cone's corner A to corner B, tucking corner D inside. Run bead of glue up the line B to C.

6. Open hanger and straighten out; cut at 15".

7. Curl 2" loop at one end of hanger. Run wire up through cone with loop on bottom. Hot glue wire to cone at "waist" (see diagram below).

52

OPPOSITE: This class clown has been
added to put a bit more humor in
our lives!

To make Accordion Body:

1. Cut out all of 2" Orange Strips and 2" Mint Strips (Page 56). You should have four strips in total to make Accordion Body. Glue two Orange Strips end to end, and two Mint Strips end to end; then fold in half lengthwise to form two 22" strips. Lay strip over strip in "L" pattern. Glue at corner, folding strip over strip, keeping your strips even as you go. Use white glue at end.

2. With awl, or nail, poke a hole straight through the center of Accordion Body; set aside.

3. Cut out two 1" strips (one orange, one mint). Cut these into ½" strips lengthwise. Do the same as Accordian Body; place in "L" pattern, glue at corner, fold over to form "Accordion Arms," and use white glue at end.

4. Cut and fold Arms paper element (Page 57) where indicated. Glue onto "Accordian Arms," then set aside.

5. Cut out Jester Hat and Pom-Poms (Page 57); you can use real Pom-Poms here if you prefer. Glue to hat with white glue.

6. Run thin bead of white glue along edges of backside of hat, leaving bottom edge free of glue, card stock; set aside to dry, then cut out.

7. Give wooden ball an extra tap on top to deepen hole; work it off the "stand."

8. Cut out Face (Page 57) or use a 1" circle punch. Cut small slits all the way around face; set aside.

9. Cut 2" by 24" strip of beige crepe paper. Use decorative scissors to cut one edge.

10. Gently stitch wide running stitch along straight edge and gather together. To seal thread to paper, use a dab of hot glue.

11. Cut 1 ½" by 24" strip of crepe paper, cutting along both edges with decorative scissors.

12. Sew running stitch down center; gather, then seal thread.

13. Begin assembling. Slide on wide ruffle next to Cone through wire; hot glue to "Accordion Body" working all the way up through all the holes.

14. Slide on neck ruffle; hot glue to body. Face hands forward and hot glue arms in place at shoulder area.

15. Glue ball to wire, utilizing hole made with stand. Put thin layer of glue on face; glue in position.

16. Open hat, then glue on.

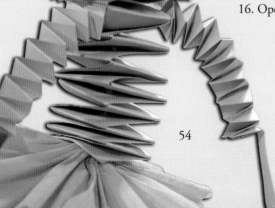

glue

glue

fold

fold

cut arms

cut arms

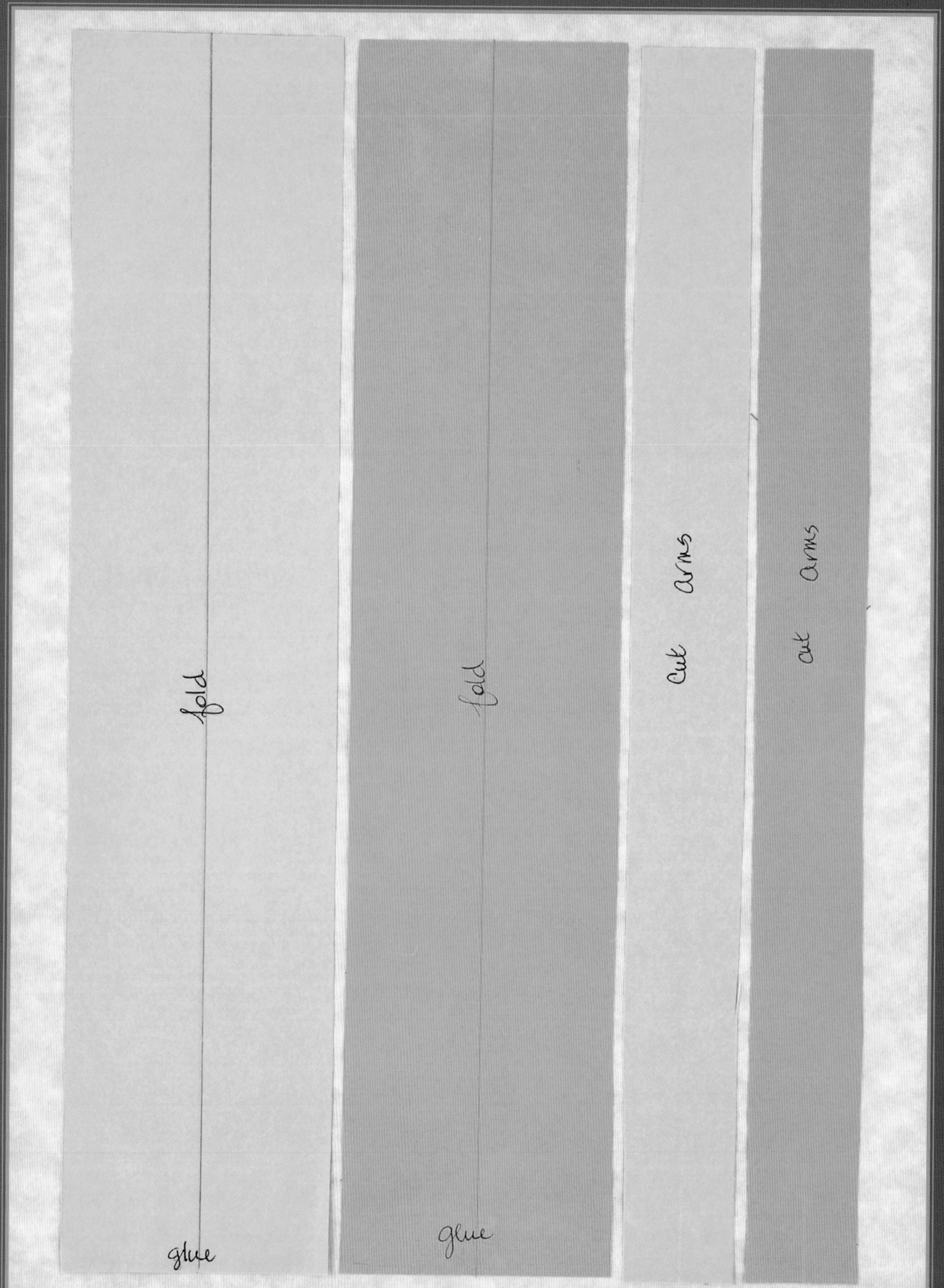

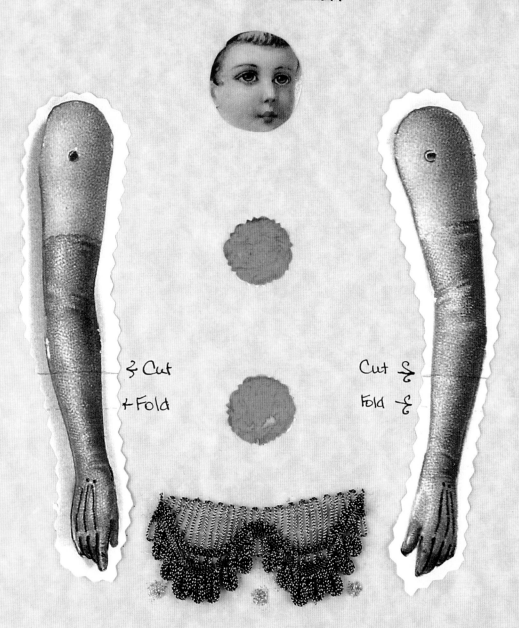

ce in which to look
gayety, yet even in A
quit all of the wit and
populace de

Cut
Fold

Cut
Fold

HIGGINS PLAYING CARD ART DOLL

"Alice in Wonderland" meets "Great Expectations." A well-worn deck of playing cards offers endless possibilities when designing an art piece. The rich detail and bright colors mixed with stark black-and-white elements make an interesting combination. The gold brass buttons on this clever guy came from an old military jacket that most likely saw many a deck of playing cards in its time.

Materials

- 24-gauge wire
- Card stock
- Hammer
- Hot glue
- Matte decoupage glue
- Rivets and rivet tool
- Wire cutters

Instructions

1. Cut out all paper elements (Pages 60, 61), then decoupage to card stock; set aside to dry, then cut out.

2. Glue neck area of head to back of body with white glue.

3. Glue face to head and hat to head.

4. Glue heart, diamond, spade and Book Print Ball paper elements to hat.

5. White glue bow to neck, hands to arms, and shoes to ankles.

6. White glue buttons to body.

7. Attach arms and legs to body with rivets.

8. If you want to hang art doll, cut a 2" piece of wire; twist into a loop and hot glue onto back of hat.

Note: Two extra illusion spheres are included (Page 61).

58

OPPOSITE: The cherubic face on the Higgins Playing Card Art Doll is anything but innocent.

Milles Bons Baisers

The delicately embroidered scrolls on this shoe came from a lovely French silk ball gown circa 1880s. The dress was so deteriorated that only a small portion of the skirt could be saved. Milles Bons Baisers, which in French means 1,000 kisses, is how the back of a turn-of-the-century postcard was signed. On the front of the postcard was the irresistible little girl you see here. She was so sweet looking that the artist thought all she needed was a pair of wings!

Materials

- ³⁄₁₆" dowel (cut to 9 ½" length)
- ½" wooden candle cup
- 1 ¹⁄₁₆" wooden finial dowel cap
- 1 ½" wooden thread spool
- 1" paintbrush
- 2" wooden circle

- Card stock
- Exacto knife
- Hot glue
- Ivory acrylic paint
- Matte decoupage glue
- Needle-nose pliers

- Opaline glitter
- Papier mâché boot
- Pink glitter
- Taupe paint
- Twine
- *Optional: ¼" hole punch*

Instructions

1. Copy Book Print paper element (Page 69) three times.

2. Copy Scrolls with Pink Dots page (Page 67) two times.

3. Paint boot (to sole area only), boot lid, wood circle, and wood finial with ivory paint; set aside to dry. Leave sole area and bottom of boot bare kraft paper.

4. Paint wood candle cup with taupe paint; set aside to dry.

5. Glue finial to wood circle and candle cup to finial.

6. Tear ivory Book Print into 1" pieces and the brown German Book Print (Page 69) into ½" pieces.

7. Decoupage entire boot and top of lid with ivory Book Print pieces.

OPPOSITE: Milles Bons Baisers was loosely inspired by Rocky and Bullwinkle's cartoon, "Fractured Fairy Tales."

8. Decoupage heel, sole, and bottom of boot with brown German Book Print pieces.

9. Cut out as many Scrolls with Pink Dots (Page 67) as you like using decorative edge scissors; decoupage onto boot, then set aside to dry.

10. With Exacto knife, cut out a 4" X on toe area of boot (see diagram at right).

11. With needle-nose pliers, gently curl out points to form starburst opening.

12. Cut first three lines of script writing, "Milles bons baisers" (Page 65), into ¾" strips with decorative scissors; glue together end to end with white glue.

13. You will need about 13" to go around boot lid; glue on with white glue.

14. Hot glue final piece to top; tie a twine bow to finial.

15. Cut out both Fairy paper elements (Pages 65-66), making sure to cut out scroll under larger Fairy.

16. Cut out tiny Pink Dots (Page 65). You can use hole punch for dots.

17. Cut out Fairy Wings (Page 65).

18. Glue wings to back of large Fairy.

19. Decoupage small "Smashed Fairy" (Page 65) and tiny dots onto sole of boot (just for giggles)!

20. Decoupage large Fairy with Scroll and Wings to card stock (Page 66); set aside to dry.

21. Hot glue thread spool inside boot with the hole at an angle (see diagram below). This will provide the base for the Fairy on the dowel.

22. Hot glue dowel to back of Fairy and Scroll, leaving 1 ½" of dowel exposed at base; insert into spool.

64

ART

Milles bons baisers
Melle Irène Mahieux
chez ses Parents
Villa St Denys
Chantilly
oise

← Cut out fairy

Pink dots

Smashed fairy
for
Underfoot!

Some extra elements

"Of all the gifts
that I might give
In one way or another,
I know you'll treasure
most these words,
I love you, my
precious Mother"

Nov., 16th, 1928

You may enjoy
adding some of
these embellishments....

Gleich lautlos und eilig durchschritt sie di
m oberen Ende die wenigen Stufen hingn in da
sie dich umbrächten, so würde das noch das Gelinde
ch aber quälten sie dich jämmerlich zu Tode, bis
übrigen sind. Jedenfalls aber, wenn du sehen mü
hausen, würdest du Streit beginnen und sie so zu

Du darfst nimmermehr hier bleiben."
ädchen ging auf den Alten zu, faßte seine Hand u
rtin, ihr denkt wohl an alles und sorgt für alle, ab
sagt, ist doch richtig, und wenn die sonst gewisse Ze
erden soll, ist es nothwendig, daß ihnen gegeb

Ich werde hier bleiben. Daß ich keinen Str
glaubt ihr wohl. Ich bin ein Kind und in Gott
s Haus hüten."
wollten fast lachen, als sie das Mädchen so red
en sahen sich erschrocken untereinander an; Bern
e rasch und fast unwillig: „Ja, du bist ein unwisse
Anne Marie, sonst würdest du nicht so albern
habe dich immer für viel klüger gehalten. Als
eb bei ihnen machte, daß du ein Kind bist. Ab
e Wüthriche nicht."
ennen? Hast du vergessen, Bernhard, wie ich hi
nun mehr als drei Jahren? Ich habe es nicht v
och ganz genau, wie die Kaiserlichen in unsere Sta
orbeten und sengten. Glaubst du, ich könnte ve
ber Vater in seiner Amtstracht in der Studierstu
erschlagen wurde? Vergebens hielt ich ihn unn
it ihm, als er zu Boden stürzte. Sterbend hat
bis jetzt hat sich sein Segen bewährt. O ich wei
mit der Mutter die Leiche des lieben Vaters au
ufe trug und bis zur Kirchhofsmauer hinter de
die Mutter mich von da wegriß, über den Mark
e, wo es überall taghell war, von den brennende
dicht an uns vorbei all das wilde, wüthende Vol
en uns, wie die Bürger unserer Stadt verwund
chlagen und niedergeschossen wurden, Männe

Wir aber gingen unberührt hindurch, als ob wi
Das war nur des Vaters Segen, dem Gott b
O! ich habe nichts davon vergessen. Nicht ver
delungen sich weiter über das Land verbreiteten,
gkeit heraus, weitere Hauptmeridiane zu ziehen.
te, zweite, dritte u. s. w. Haupt-Meridian. Recogn
ten Range, so giebt man zugleich die Nummer
an, zu dessen System er gehört. Da unser Fre
Busche von Ober-Wisconsin haust, so ist die
andes in der Weise zu vervollständigen, daß man
hauptmeridians nennt, der durch Wisconsin
n läuft. Es ist der vierte.
Fällen wurden die Meridiane nicht numerirt, son
amen belegt, so giebt es einen Michigan-Merit
Boise-Meridian in Idaho u. s. w.
sei hier noch erwähnt, daß der sechste Meridian
im Staate Nebraska durchschneidet. Der gröz
Jowa, Missouri und Arkansas liegt westlich
ridian. Mit den Meridianen mehrten sich se
undlinien, da beide zusammen gleichsam ein Syf
r Grundlinien bildet z. B. die Grenze zwischen
d Nebraska.
so, daß ein Township, etwa wegen eines größe
ollständig hergestellt werden kann, so nennt man
es Township ein gebrochenes (Fraction
ck gebraucht man auch für eine unvollständ
vollständige Unterabtheilung einer Section.
nwachsende Geschlecht hat die Regierung in nobe
a jedem Township wird eine Section, und zwar
r Volksschulzwecke reservirt.
t der Hans seine Aufgabe gelöst zu haben.
für dieses Mal nicht nieder, ohne seinen Lese
en beim Antritt des neuen Jahres zu wünsch

and on another occasion, "I do not approve," he said
e condemnation in Fénelon, of those whom he is ple
call mystics—to which persuasion I belong." In
ese curious spiritual intimations of his were in the
re of direct mystical experience. They did not lead
adopt a thorough-going mystical philosophy; for
me too seldom and too fleetingly for him to feel
pressure and tradition of the society of which
members. It was made all the more difficult by the fact
of contemplation was to act in opposition to the
role, function, responsibilities. For them, to take up a lif
as much as to a royal prince, was allotted a ready-made
aristocratic government and social life; to them, almost
were integral and active parts of the great machine of
self. But future peers in that day were not free. They
writing in which he could most fully have expressed him-
ience and devote himself to that life of thought and
why he should not break away from conventional exist-
no practical reason—if he had ever felt the inclination—
best course for his talents. As a younger son there was
since he was a child, had hampered him in following the
before, entangled in the web of that worldly life which,
thankful for. He was now, even more inextricably than
and a large fortune. It was not in reality anything to be
were they had ever seriously influenced mank
were entirely reversed; he was now the heir to a peerage
aphael was employed to decorate the Vatican"

For William the event was momentous. His prospects

vied by men and courted by women, recognized and
pleasures and privileges. They walked through life en-
one. With some of the duties of royalty they had all its
that the position imposed on them was such an attractive

ir different ways, the apex of Whig civilization. In
all that made it memorable found its fullest expres-
Holland House showed its masculine and intel-
l side. Lady Holland was a divorced woman: she
loped with Lord Holland from her first husband, for
Godfrey Webster. With the consequence that,
gh the easy-going circle of Lady Melbourne
Duchess of Devonshire were on terms w
never received by the more rigid ladies; and the
y that visited her was predominantly male. Every
of the week gentlemen used to drive down through
reen fields of Kensington to dine and sleep at Hol-
House. Staying there had its drawbacks. It could
onizingly cold for one thing; and the dinner table
always overcrowded, so that people ate as best
could, with arms glued to their sides. Moreover
Holland he
Holland he was in many respects a tiresome
an, capricious, mineering and extremely egotistic;
to a hundred deliberately cultivated fads, with
h she expected everyone to fall in. She shifted her
s' places in the middle of a meal, she turned people
f the room for using scent, she interrupted, she had

onvincing reality as long as they lasted. And th
ey did not displace his rationalism, they underm
security. Uneasily he hung suspended between
inions.

No wonder he was paradoxical! What was life b
No wonder he was iron
ndle of contradictions?
ced by the preposterous incongruity of experience,
sily thing a reasonable person could do was to s
shoulders and smile. His duality of vision appear
attitude to every sort of subject. No one appreci
ter the achievements of culture: but he did not

they were integral and active parts
THE BEAU MONDE
LOVE

Flora Fairies—Lolly

During a visit with her husband's family in upstate New York, Sandra's mother-in-law, Barbara, brought out a wonderful old scrapbook. It had belonged to David's grandmother, Pearl, who as a child filled her days collecting advertising and business cards from the salesmen who made visits to her father's store. Sandra, an ephemera fanatic, couldn't believe her eyes—and the pages of brightly colored cards. The scrapbook was hers to take home, and needless to say, the artist went through quite a bit of copier ink after that. Details of these papers helped this fairy take wing.

Materials

- 19-gauge wire
- 3-D foam dots
- Card stock
- Decorative edge scissors
- Matte decoupage glue
- Opaline glitter
- Wire cutters

  Optional: Lace or netting

Instructions

1. Roughly cut out all paper elements (Pages 72-75) and decoupage to card stock; set aside to dry, then cut out precisely.

2. Use decorative scissors for Script Back Wings (Page 75) and Fairy's Tail (Page 74) paper elements.

3. Assemble body; glue together with white glue.

4. Use 3-D foam dots under flower "skirt" (Page 72) and flower "top" (Page 72).

5. Use foam dots between Polka Dot Wings (Page 73) and Script Back Wings, one for tail, and also to put hat and shoes on.

6. Cut wire to 2" piece. Make wire loop and hot glue to top back of Paper Ribbon (Page 75) for hanging. Add touches of opaline glitter to tail.

   Optional: Embellish with lace or netting or additional paper elements provided.

OPPOSITE: The demure little face on a baking soda advertising card was the perfect choice for this fairy. Do fairies have tails? Sandra's do!

Mystiques Voix de France
La Sainte qui sut protéger Paris
Sauvera bien le reste du Pays.

You can make color copies of vintage ribbon for tails too!

Do fairies have tails? Mine do!

Tarts Business Card Art Dolls

There are so many alluring business cards with such beautiful artwork, and Sandra can't seem to toss a single one out. Too lovely to tuck away in a drawer, the cards are incorporated into the artist's pieces. Some wind up as collage borders, while the prettiest ones turn into these animated maidens—constant reminders of Sandra's favorite places to shop!

Materials

- Blue crepe paper
- Card stock
- Decorative edge scissors
- Hot glue
- Matte decoupage glue
- Peach crepe paper
- Pink crepe paper
- White glue

Instructions

1. Cut out Round Head paper elements (Pages 78, 80, 82) with decorative edge scissors.

2. Cut out Torso, including Arms, paper elements (Pages 78, 80, 82). Be sure to cut out neck and tab area. Decoupage all to card stock.

3. Cut out Buttons, Black-and-White Pinwheel, and Spiral paper elements (Pages 78, 80, 82, 83); glue to skirts. Cut out skirts (Pages 79, 81, 83). Use decorative edge scissors on "hem" area. Decoupage to card stock; let dry.

4. On skirts, hot glue corner (A) to corner (B), tucking (D) inside.

5. Run a bead of hot glue up the line (B) to (C).

6. Hot glue Head and Arms onto Torso piece (position any way you like).

7. Slide Torso into skirt cone.

8. Make your own crepe paper aprons or fashion a wide waistband and bow.

9. Fashion florettes out of crepe paper for hat.

OPPOSITE: Tarts Business Card Art Dolls would make beguiling place card holders at an afternoon tea party.

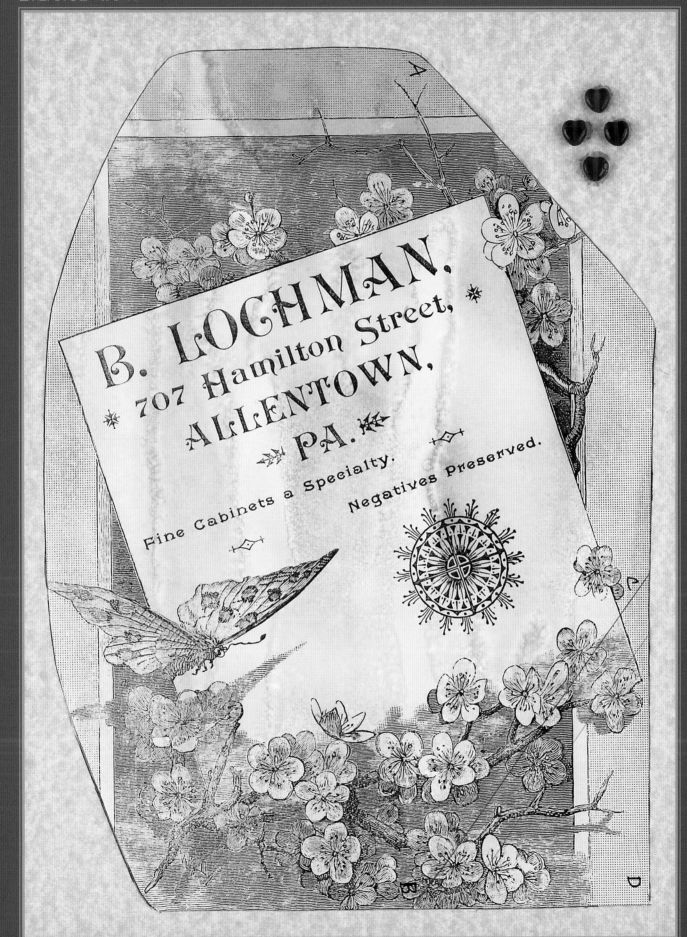

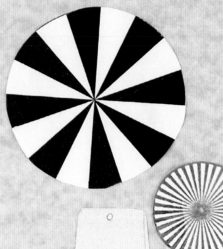

"THE "TROJAN"
Fine Linen Collars
- are unequaled.

PARIS
FLEA
MARKET
POSH LITTLE FOLLIES
BY
SANDRA EVERTSON
ARTIST • DESIGNER

www.Shabbytiques.com

TAB

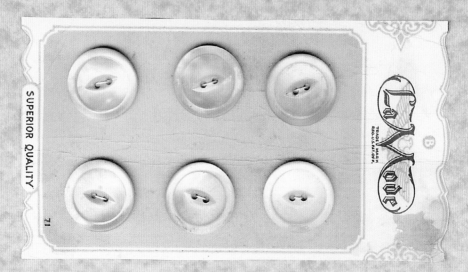

SUPERIOR QUALITY

71

Kimberly Stanier

Judy Watkins

Antiques, Gifts & Home Embellishments

Antiques, Gifts & Home Embellishments

CALA

San Luis Obispo

Antiques, Gifts & Home Embellishments

Tab

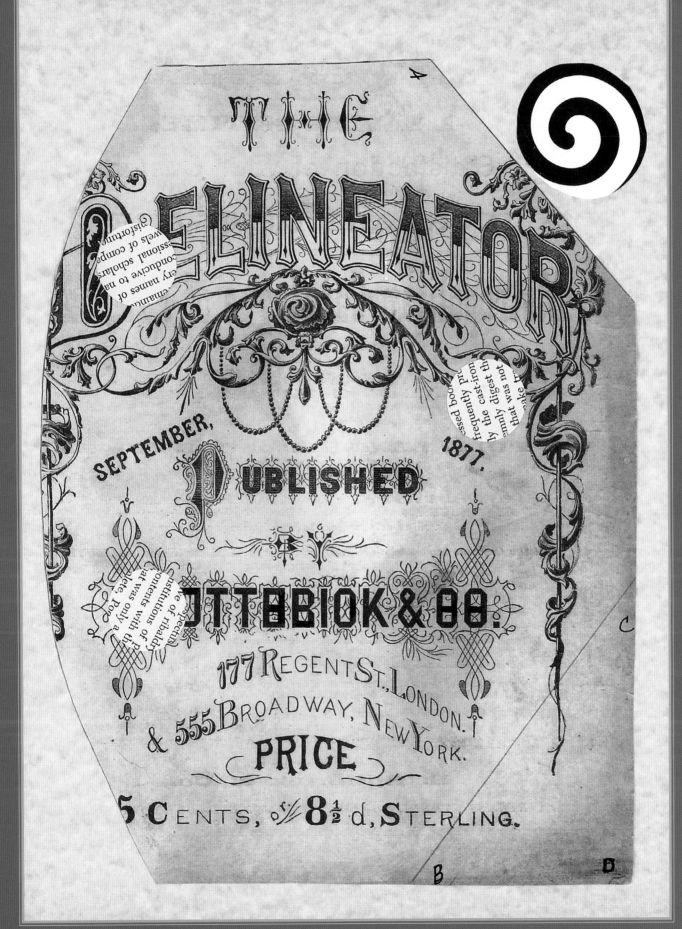

PETITE THEATRE

A friend came across an 1870s German almanac and presented it to Sandra as a gift. The pages are so brittle and brown that it couldn't possibly last much longer. Slowly but surely, the artist is copying each page in an effort to preserve its beauty. Among its pages Sandra has found novelties ranging from number puzzles and letter games to recipes and planting calendars. This is where the German print used on this theatre came from.

Materials

- 1 clear glass 6mm bead
- 1 colored glass 4mm bead
- 19-gauge wire
- 2 ½" by 3 ¼" by 4 ½" rectangular kraft box (ivory, if available)
- 2" by 3" craft mirror

- Card stock
- Decorative edge scissors
- Exacto knife
- Ivory paint
- Jewelry findings
- Matte decoupage glue

- Needle-nose pliers
- Wire cutters

  Optional: Peach crepe paper, netting, lace, feathers, needle and thread

Instructions

To make theatre:

1. Cut out Exterior Back of Box paper element (Page 89); decoupage onto back of box.

2. Cut out two 2 ½" by 10" strips of large German Book Print paper element (Page 90) for exterior sides; decoupage on. (You will have a bit left over since you only need 15" to go all the way around.)

3. Cover seams with Exterior and Trim pieces (Page 87); use decorative scissors to cut out.

4. Cut out Front Panel paper element (Page 87).

5. Using Exacto knife, cut center oval out of Front Panel; fit to top of box and trace oval center onto box lid. Using an Exacto knife again, cut oval out on the box top. To make hole smooth, rub white glue along edge. Smooth with fingertip; set aside to dry.

6. Decoupage Front Panel onto front of box.

OPPOSITE: A statuesque ballerina is the star of the show in this Petite Theatre.

7. Cut out three ½" strips of Alphabet Print element (Page 88) for lid side trim; glue together end to end. Cut one edge with decorative scissors. You will need 15" to go all the way around box top lid exterior. Glue on.

8. Cut out Interior Box Top Lid paper element (Page 88). Trace oval onto it and cut out center; decoupage on.

9. Cut out Floor, Ceiling, Side Walls, and Drapes paper elements (Pages 87, 89).

10. Decoupage drapes to card stock; set aside to dry.

11. Decoupage Side Walls and Ceiling in place.

12. Cut small "T" slit in center of floor (A) for tab placement later; set aside.

(A)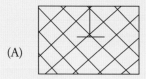

To make Ballerina:

1. Cut out Ballerina, dotted Ballerina Backing, and Tutu Front and Tutu Back paper elements (Pages 87, 88). Use decorative scissors for "hem" of Tutu. *Optional: Here you may choose to make your own skirt.*

2. Use crepe paper, netting, or lace to embellish skirt. You will need a piece about ½" by 8".

3. Cut piece of card stock the size of dotted Ballerina Backing and decoupage backing to card stock. Rough cut Ballerina and decoupage onto other side of dotted Ballerina Backing; set aside to dry, then cut out entire piece. Be sure to cut out tab area, too.

4. Finish Ballerina with feather on top, if you desire.

To finish theatre:

1. Cut out center of Drapes paper element (Page 89) and hot glue to mirror. Glue entire piece in place on back wall.

2. Make small hole in center of ceiling for "chandelier."

3. Cut 2" piece of wire. Curl a loop at one end, slide on bead and jewelry finding, then slip through hole from inside up. Slide on jewelry finding and bead, then curl end closed.

4. Hot glue Ballerina in place, then decoupage floor (Page 87) in place (make sure "T" slit is in back).

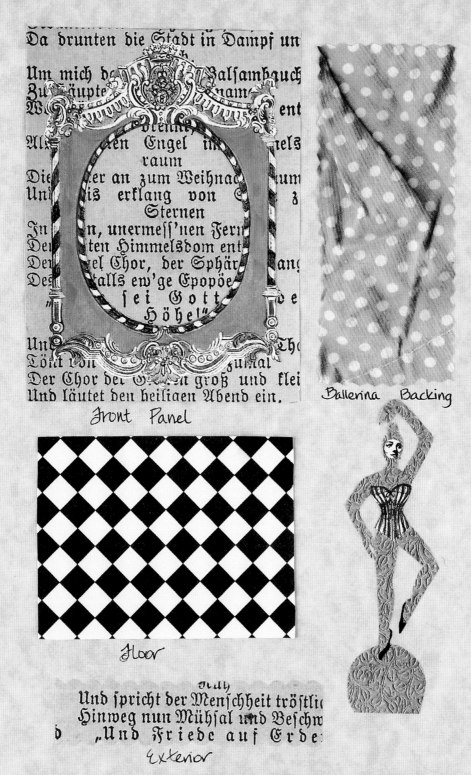

Da brunten die Stadt in Dampf un

Um mich de̲ ̲ ̲ ̲ ̲Balſambauch
Zu Häupte̲ ̲ ̲ ̲nam̲ ̲ ̲ ̲ ̲
W̲ ̲ ̲ ̲ ̲ ̲ ̲ ̲ ̲ ̲ ̲ent
b̲renni,̲ ̲ ̲
Als̲ ̲ ̲ ̲en Engel im̲ ̲ ̲els̲
raum
Die̲ ̲er an zum Weihnac̲ ̲ ̲um
Un̲ ̲ ̲is erklang von̲ ̲ ̲ ̲ ̲z̲
Sternen
In̲ ̲ ̲n, unermeſſ'nen Fern̲
De̲ ̲ ̲ten Himmelsdom ent̲
De̲ ̲ ̲el Chor, der Sphär̲ ̲ang̲
De̲ ̲ ̲alls ew'ge Epopöe
̲ ̲ ̲ ̲ ̲ſei Gott̲ ̲ ̲ ̲ ̲e̲
Höhe!"

Un̲ ̲ ̲ ̲ ̲ ̲ ̲ ̲ ̲ ̲ ̲Th̲
Tönt̲ ̲on̲ ̲ ̲ ̲ ̲ ̲ ̲ ̲ ̲umal
Der Chor der̲ ̲ ̲ ̲en groß und klei̲
Und läutet den heiligen Abend ein.

Front Panel

Ballerina Backing

Floor

Und spricht der Menſchheit tröſtli̲
Hinweg nun Mühſal und Beſchw̲
d ̲ ̲ ̲ ̲ "Und Friede auf Erde̲

Exterior

es̲ ̲ ̲ ̲ ̲ ̲ ̲ ̲ ̲ ̲ ̲ ̲
Friedſelig über die Stadt einher,
Umfluthet alle die dunkeln Dächer,
Die hohen Giebel, die niedern

Trim

ABCDOEEFGHIKLM

MNOPQRSTUVXYZ

MNOPQRSTUVXYZ

ABCDOEEFGHIKLM

Lid Side Trim

Tutu Front

Tutu Back

Interior Box Top
Lid

Drapes

Cut
out
this part

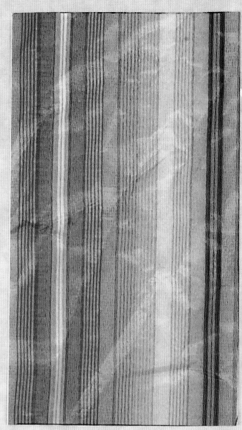

Side Walls
(Copy wall twice)

Exterior Back of Box

Ceiling

ENLARGE 118%

Nacht,

mit Menſchen zu fr

heiligen N

llen Gaſſen ein fröh

eſtlicher Glanz durch

hen,

iedrigſten Haus durch

Ritzen

ich die Lichter des

blitzen,

auſche hinein und ſch

Tiſch

Exterior Sides

Vintage
Ribbon #

Some of
my
favorite
ribbons
you might
enjoy adding
to your
theater.

BABBIT'S CABBAGE

Scouring flea markets, Sandra comes across some interesting things, like a whole package of bright "grass green" crepe papers circa 1920. Not too unusual until the artist noticed a note taped onto the front of the package that read: "I'm sure you'll have great fun with this. I love you, I love you truly, Ruby!" What else could Sandra do but follow the advice? A fat green cabbage is what came to mind.

Materials

- 19-gauge wire
- 2 ½" round papier mâché ornament
- Bleach
- Card stock
- Cotton swab

- Decorative edge scissors
- Exacto knife
- Green crepe paper
- Hot glue
- Matte decoupage glue

- Needle-nose pliers
- Toothpick
- Water
- White glue
- Wire cutters

Instructions

To make cabbage base:

1. Cut little more than ¾" off top of ornament (this becomes a "cup").

2. Hot glue cut portion to bottom of ball for stand (A).

   (A)

3. Decoupage entire "cup" inside and out with ½" pieces of Book Print (Page 97); set aside to dry.

4. You will need about 50 to 60 crepe paper cabbage leaves. To expedite this, fold crepe paper into 2" sections several times; place Cabbage Leaf Pattern (Page 96) on top and cut out.

5. With toothpick, begin rolling leaves at rounded edge, tightly around toothpick; loosen a bit when you get to flat edge to release toothpick, then slide it out. Leave leaf curled in tight little roll while you do all the rest. (This helps to set the curl.)

6. Starting at the bottom and working your way up, glue leaves around the cup; let dry. To get a variegated look on the leaves, mix ½ water and ½ bleach, then place a few drops on the leaves with a cotton swab.

OPPOSITE: Sitting on a head of cabbage, Babbit the rabbit invites you to a special party.

To make rabbit:

1. Roughly cut out Rabbit and Invitation paper element (Page 95). Decoupage Rabbit and Invitation to card stock.

2. Decoupage Burlap backing (Page 98) to back area of Rabbit; set aside to dry, then precisely cut out.

3. Cut out Dots paper elements (Page 96) then decoupage to each other with card stock in between. The red dot with white pattern is a "wire cover" for the back of the Rabbit. Decoupage it to card stock, then cut out.

4. Cut 16" piece of wire; make small swirl on one end (B). Make about five 2" spirals and make another swirl at top; bend top swirl vertically (C). This entire piece of wire spiral should be about 4 ¼" tall.

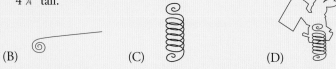

(B)   (C)   (D)

5. Hot glue top swirl wire to Rabbit back (D). Do this by laying Rabbit flat then placing dab of glue on Rabbit back. Set in vertical wire swirl then finish with "wire cover" dot.

6. Hot glue remaining dots in place: red and black dot behind tail, black and brown dot behind hat, and striped dot in front of sign. Extra dot is provided; place where you prefer.

To assemble:

Hot glue wire spiral to interior cabbage base. Add Blooms paper elements (Page 99) to the base if you prefer.

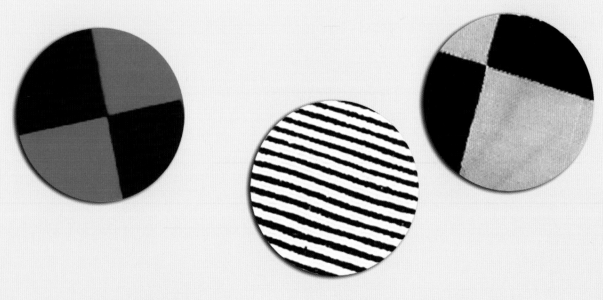

Cut out Rabbit
& Invitation

serenity

happiness

Cabbage
leaf pattern

NE W
BY

SOLIDS
OLD

The Good

The Good

beauty

happiness

serenity

Burlap Backing

So you don't
have to hunt ~
here are some
little blooms for
the base.

POSIES

Family is a very important part of Sandra's life. She treasures her relationships, especially the close bond she shares with her mother, Mary. Her mother is one of five sisters—Mary, Helen, Carmen, Jane, and Connie. They are the inspiration for these dainty posies. All beautiful, and each very unique. The flapper girl's face came from a cosmetic ad for Rosey Red Rouge.

Materials

- ¼" hole punch
- 2" terra-cotta pots
- Card stock
- Crepe paper
- Decorative edge scissors
- Floral foam
- Hot glue
- Matte decoupage glue
- Moss
- Pipe cleaners
- Ribbon
- Rivets and rivet tool
- White Glue

Optional: Pom-poms, stamen

Instructions

Note: Enough elements have been provided to make three Posies.

1. Cut out Posie Petal Backing (Page 102) and decoupage to card stock; set aside to dry, then cut out using decorative scissors.

2. Cut out faces into 1 ¼" circles (Page 102), leaving a bit of the "rays" showing.

3. Cut out Book Print "doilies," leaf hands, and tags (Pages 102, 103) and decoupage to card stock; set aside to dry, then cut out. Use ¼" hole punch for tags.

4. Dab hot glue into the terra-cotta pot and glue in piece of floral foam; set aside.

5. Using crepe paper petal folding technique (see Page 22, #12, #13), cut out and curl 25-30 crepe paper petals (with the artwork facing down on Posie Petal Backing). Starting on the perimeter, about 1" in, glue on one ring of petals with white glue.

6. Twist two different colored pipe cleaners together to form the stem; cut pipe cleaners to 7 ½" tall; hot glue to center inside first ring of petals.

7. About 1" down from top of stem, hot glue 3 ½" single pipe cleaners for arms.

8. Continue gluing on petals, then hot glue on "doily" (can add pom-poms and stamen here). Glue face on top of that. Hot glue two leaves together with about 1" of pipe cleaner sandwiched between to form hands. Apply rivets and ribbons to tags; hot glue to leaf hands.

9. Finish with a bit of moss to cover floral foam.

100

OPPOSITE: No watering required for these coquettish little posies.

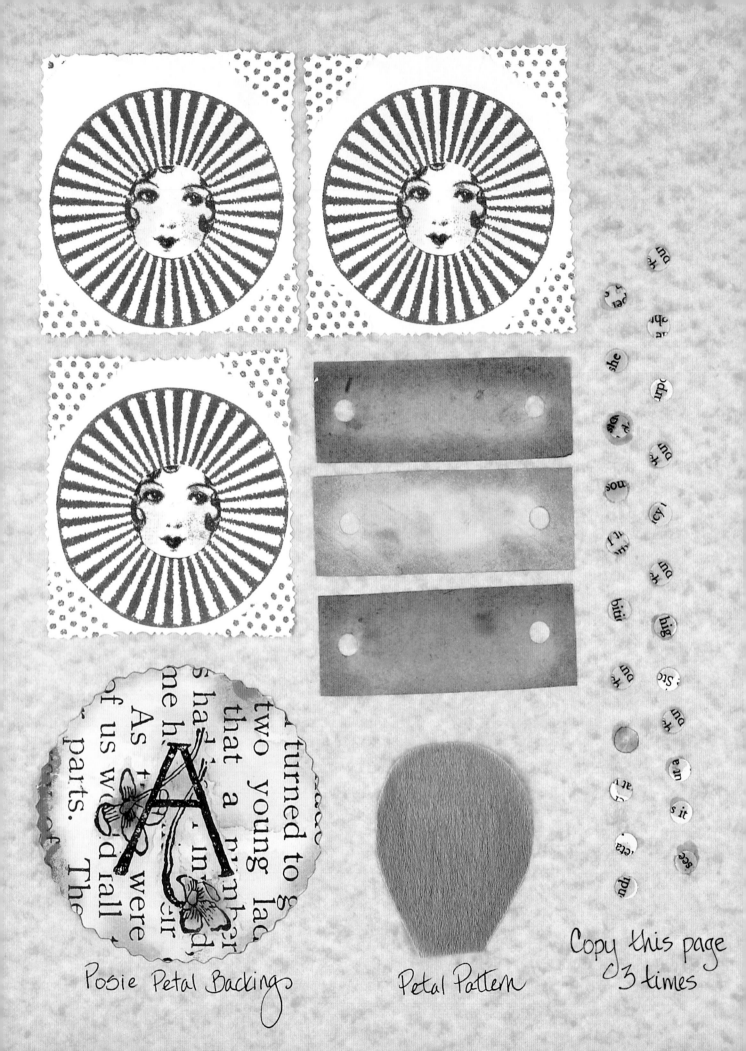

Posie Petal Backings

Petal Pattern

Copy this page 3 times

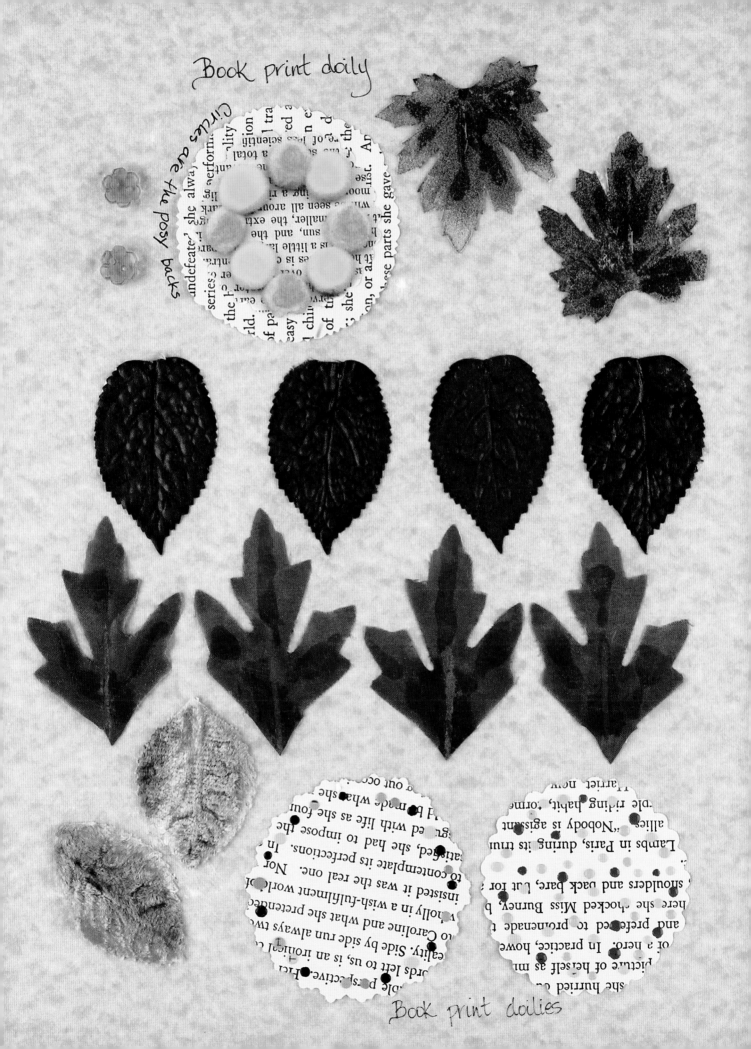

Book print doily

Circles are the posy backs

Book print doilies

TEMPUS FUGIT

Included in Sandra's archive of antique books is a turn-of-the-century merchandise catalog in which you could mail order just about anything. The clock face on Tempus Fugit came from this catalog, while the fabric came from a small cache of scraps saved from childhood clothes Sandra's mother had made. The sunny yellow and orange 1960s fabric was used to make a very hip bellbottom jumpsuit with a reversible floppy brimmed hat.

Materials

- ¼" drill bit
- ¼" hole punch
- 1 ¼" wooden ball
- 3 ¾" round papier mâché disk ornament
- 22-gauge copper wire

- Black paint pen
- Copper glitter
- Drill
- Hot glue
- Matte decoupage glue
- Pencil

- Popsicle stick
- Two ¼" wooden dowels
- Two 1 ½" wooden egg halves
- White glue
- Wire cutters

  Optional: Ribbon

Instructions

To make body:

1. Remove string from disk ornament.

2. Drill one ¼" hole on top surface of each egg half.

3. Cut two pieces of dowel 7 ½" tall. Hot glue dowel to egg halves.

4. Make two holes in disk edge about 1 ½" apart; apply white glue and insert dowels as far upwards as possible. Add a bit of hot glue at hole entrance; set aside to dry thoroughly.

5. Hot glue wooden ball on top.

6. Paint stripes on legs with black paint pen.

7. Cut out clock face (Page 107), then decoupage in place on round disk.

8. Cut out center dial (Page 107), then decoupage on.

OPPOSITE: Old clothes may be long gone but not forgotten. On the backside of Tempus Fugit, or, time flies, remnant copies of the artist's childhood clothes serve as circular embellishments.

9. Cut out Face paper element (Page 107). Cut slits all the way around (see diagram at right), Decoupage onto wooden ball then smooth down edges with Popsicle stick.

10. Cut out Arms, Bow Tie, Stars, and Dots paper elements (Pages 107, 108). Decoupage to card stock. On arms, decoupage front to card stock; set aside to dry, cut out, then decoupage Book Print Arm (Page 108) on other side with card stock sandwiched between. You will do the same with the Top Hat Brim elements.

To make stove pipe top hat:

1. Cut out Top Hat paper elements (Page 109) and decoupage to card stock; set aside to dry, then cut out.

2. Using hot glue, make a tube of top hat "stove pipe" (A).

3. Cut out center hole from outer brim, then cut ¼" slits up to score area (B). Fold up (C).

4. Cut ¼" slits on top of hat to score area (D). Fold down (E).

5. Hot glue top of hat inside "stove pipe tube" with slits on inside.

6. Glue brim of hat inside "stove pipe tube" with slits on the inside.

7. Decoupage Dr. Blumers Hat Band paper element (Page 108) in position.

8. Glue hat to head.

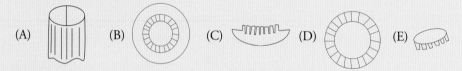

To finish body:

1. Cut out and apply Side Trim (Page 108) on disk and Shoe Buttons (Page 109) with white glue.

2. Glue arms in place about ⁷⁄₁₆" from edge. This will give the piece extra stability.

3. Cut out Cartoon Back circle (Page 108) and decoupage onto back of body, covering arms.

4. Glue Bow Tie (Page 107) in place or use a ribbon instead.

5. Cut 20" piece of copper wire. Form a loop on both ends (A).

6. Wrap wire around pencil, about 30 times. Remove pencil, lay "spring" flat on counter, then flatten down with a book (B).

7. Shape into an arch and adjust to your liking.

8. Hot glue Stars (Page 107) to front of spring and use Dots (Page 107) to cover glue dabs behind stars.

9. Embellish with more glitter on stars.

Front

Back

Big Bow!

Center
Dial

Seeing
Stars!

Front

Back

I love ❤ to wonder who Dr. Blumer was !?

Side Trim

Side Trim

Dr Blumers

that of any other animal. Its head is about one-fourth the length of its body and, in the case of a father whale, may be twenty feet long. Its mouth extends lengthwise at the bottom of its head, and it has a narrow lower jaw.

The whale's eyes are back of its mouth, one on each side of its head, very far apart. These eyes cannot be moved as you move yours, and hence the whale cannot see very well. All that it can do is to look to the right side with its right eye and

Bottom

Hats off!

nding him fro... , why a chimney would... rpose as well as the moon. not far to seek. In the dayt... air around the sun is so brigh... ed that it is impossible to see an... the immediate neighborhood of tha... We may cut off the sunlight fro... by a chimney, but we cannot c... lumination of the air except by... above the air. The size and... e moon are such that it cu... f light for hundreds... ables us to see

Top of Hat

to stand straigh... r and turn its body often does... especially wh... ship, wh... s it to be they are... are also ly small openings, but on... to see. With these ears... g up sounds sever... for its

Topside Brim

...k of its mouth, ...n the outside they a... ...the inside they are very ...e whale... ar well, miles av... result of heari... e part thr... which it ts head near the front ...hen the nose part ...were to h...

Bottomside Brim

1, 2 Buckle My Shoe!

Shoe
Buttons

1ST

5

3RD

PIPSQUEAK

This is certainly the most involved of the projects, but also the most outstanding. It's an absolute celebration in a box! The Sulpher advertisement came from an old Ladies Home Journal circa 1894. It reminded Sandra of a traveling medicine show, where you could buy everything, from vitamins, tonics, and perfume oils to pots and pans. Step right up!

Materials

- 2 ½" round papier mâché ornament
- 22-gauge wire
- 3 ¼" height by 4" depth by 5 ¾" length papier mâché box with gold latch
- 3" round papier mâché box *(glue lid on)*
- 5" x ⅞" diameter coil for body *(available at hardware store)*
- Blue crepe paper
- Card stock
- Gray acrylic paint
- Hot glue
- Popsicle stick
- Tack
- White glue

Instructions

1. Remove latches from box; set aside.

2. Copy Blue Diamonds page three times (Page 116).
Note: To keep this piece consistent, work with diamonds horizontally.

3. Cut one 4" by 5 ¾" rectangle from Blue Diamonds paper. Decoupage onto exterior box top lid.

4. Cut out two ¾" by 5 ¾" strips from Blue Diamonds paper. Decoupage to lid front and back. Poke holes with tack where paper covers screw holes.

5. Cut out two ¾" by 4" strips from Blue Diamonds paper; decoupage onto exterior box lid sides. Brown kraft paper shows between pieces, which is part of design.

6. Cut two 2 ½" by 5 ¾" strips from Blue Diamonds paper; decoupage onto front exterior and back exterior. Poke holes with tack where paper covers screw holes.

7. Cut out two 2 ½" by 4" strips of Blue Diamonds paper for exterior sides of box; decoupage onto box.

8. Cut out Gray Balls with Stars and Clock Face paper element (Page 114). Leave one large ball for interior.

9. Decoupage Clock Face to front of box. Decoupage balls on exterior at random.

10. Re-attach latches, adding dab of white glue in screw holes.

OPPOSITE: This fanciful medicine man-in-a-box is reminiscent of a traveling salesman who peddled tonics and other cure-alls.

11. Cut out and decoupage Box Interior paper element (Page 115) in place, then Interior Bottom Back (Page 113). Cut Interior Sides where indicated (Page 113); decoupage onto box.

12. Decoupage Interior Top Sides, Interior Top "Hinge" Edge, and Interior Top Latch Edge onto box.

13. Hot glue papier mâché ball ornament to coil. Remove string. Paint ball gray; set aside to dry.

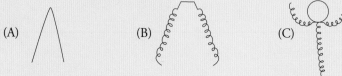

14. Cut piece of wire 25" long; bend in half (A). Coil each piece of wire around a pencil, making each arm 4" long. Leave a 1" gap in the middle (B). Hot glue coil to neck area (C).

15. Cut out Face paper element (Page 113). Cut tiny slits all the way around it.

16. Put thin layer of decoupage on face, starting at center and working outward; apply to ball. Use Popsicle stick to smooth out wrinkles.

17. Cut out Hands paper elements (Page 113) and decoupage to card stock; set aside to dry. Cut out and hot glue in place on arm coils; set aside.

18. The 3" round box will become base for Medicine Salesman. Hot glue its lid onto box.

19. Use box as a pattern to cut 3" round piece from White Dot paper element (Page 114). Decoupage to 3" round box top; set aside to dry.

20. Poke small hole in center of round box to fit coil into. Run 1" of coil down into box, sliding into hole and twisting slowly down and in. Hot glue entire piece to bottom of box.

21. Decoupage Yo-Yo's (Page 113) onto card stock, cut into stars with Star Pattern, hot glue into place.

22. Cut out large Dotted, Striped Balls (Page 113), decoupage onto card stock. When dry, cut into "coils" following pattern (Page 115). Hot glue into place. Decoupage small Dotted, Striped Balls (Page 113) to card stock; set aside to dry. Cut out and glue into place.

To make top hat:

1. Cut out Stove Pipe Hat paper elements (Page 114) and decoupage to card stock; set aside to dry, then cut out. Using hot glue, make tube of top hat "stove pipe" (A).

2. Cut out center hole from outer brim; cut ¼" slits up to score area (B). Fold up (C).

3. Cut ¼" slits on top of hat to score area (D). Fold down (E).

4. Hot glue top of hat inside stove pipe tube with slits on inside (F). Do the same for brim. Hot glue hat to head.

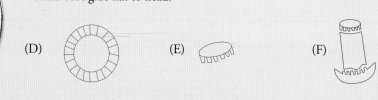

cut

Interior Sides

Interior Bottom Back

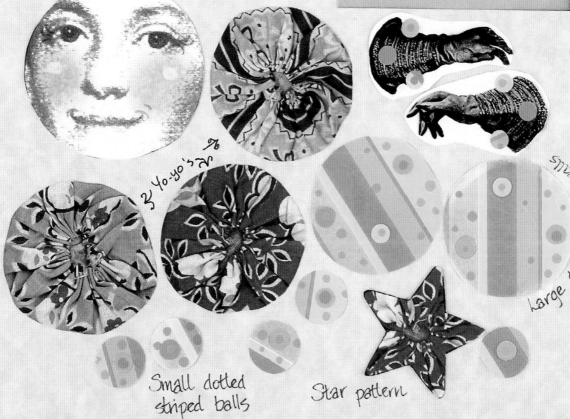

Yo-yo's

Large dotted striped balls

Small dotted striped balls

Star pattern

Stove Pipe Hat

Template

Template

Outer Brim

Top of Hat

GLENN'S

A HEALTHFUL SKIN.

SULPHUR SOAP

IS Marvelously Efficient in clearing the Skin of Impurities, and keeping it in a perfect state of health.

IT BEAUTIFIES THE COMPLEXION, while as a *Healing* agent for *Sores* or *Wounds* it passes all praise

There is no Form of uptive sease for which this Renowned Soap has not proved *efficacious.*

IN THE BATH IT IS AS BENEFICIAL AS THE WATERS OF THE RENOWNED SULPHUR SPRINGS.

REMOVES

CURES ALL OBSTINATE SKIN

Box Interior

Coil Pattern Guide

Interior Top Sides

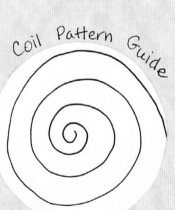

Template

Interior Top Hinge Edge

Interior Top Latch Edge

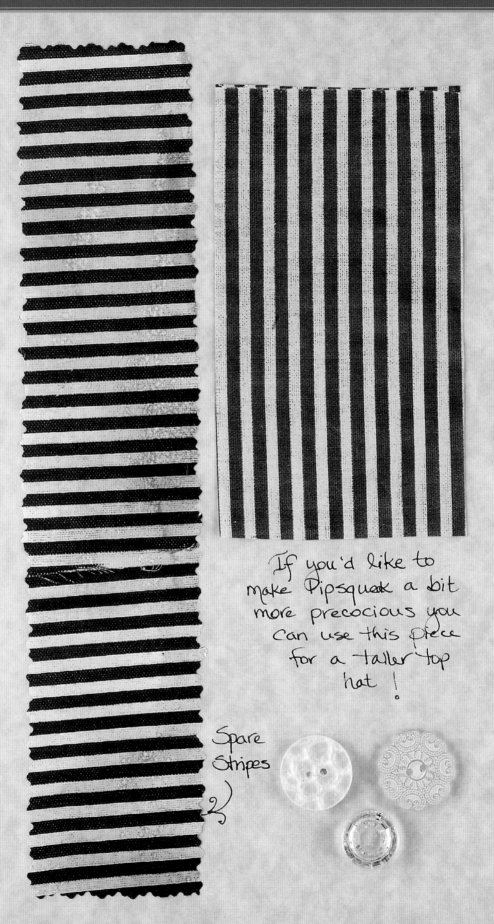

If you'd like to
make Pipsqueak a bit
more precocious you
can use this piece
for a taller top
hat !

Spare
Stripes

GIBBERISH BANDBOX

Among all the things Sandra likes to collect, vintage clothing is a particular favorite. The artist has several antique dress forms, all wearing a ravishing wardrobe. While in a small thrift shop in London, Sandra purchased a man's three-piece tuxedo circa 1870s in great condition that came with a bent-tip stiff collar, silk bow tie, and lovely glass cuff links. Much to her surprise, when she got home and unpacked it, she found a beautiful old pocket watch in one of the vest pockets and in the other pocket was a witty, brightly colored silk handkerchief with big red and blue dots on it!

Materials

- 1" craft paintbrush
- 19-gauge wire
- 2 ½" by 4 ¼" round kraft box (ivory, if available)
- 2 ½" round ball papier mâché ornament
- Clear cellophane
- Hot glue
- Ivory acrylic paint
- Matte decoupage glue
- Pool blue acrylic paint
- Popsicle stick
- Wire cutters

Instructions

1. Cut out Cone Hat and Red Stars paper elements (Page 121); decoupage to card stock.

2. Remove hanging string and paint papier mâché ornament pool blue.

3. Cut out all other paper elements (Pages 121, 122). Glue two Polka Dot strips together (Page 122) end to end to make one long 14" strip; decoupage to box. Cover two seams with Book Print Strips (Page 121).

4. Repeat with two Black-and-White Trim Strips (Page 122); decoupage to side of lid.

5. Decoupage Scroll round paper element (Page 121) to box top.

6. Hot glue ball to box top.

7. Cut tiny slits all the way around face element; decoupage face to ball, smoothing any wrinkles gently with Popsicle stick.

118

OPPOSITE: This whimsical jester's piece makes a fabulous container for confections.

8. Cut out and hot glue Cone Hat (Page 121) together. Cut out Red Stars (Page 121) and glue to hat.

9. Cut six 4" wide by 8" long cellophane rectangles (A).

10. Cut six 4" wire pieces; fold in half (B). Scrunch up cellophane down center of wire; hold the cellophane at top of wire and twist wire together (C).

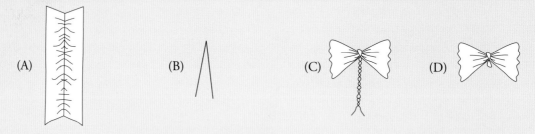

(A)   (B)   (C)   (D)

11. Curl wire "stem" into a loop (D).

12. Cut 8" piece of wire and string five of the cellophane pom-poms onto the wire (E).

(E)

13. Wrap this around the neck, even out ruffles, twist wire together, then clip off.

14. Hot glue last cellophane pom-pom to top of hat. Attach hat to head with hot glue.

Vintage Trim just for fun!

BYRON

this ball that Lady
—of indifferent memory
y London was ringing with
dying season; and such a scandal!
was just what was needed to re
was told and re-told, each time with
detail added; letters of condolence p
raged Lamb family; a scurrilous pap
published a leading article on the subject.
ew so violent that it became impossible for C
aain in London. She was packed off to spe
the summer at Brocket. Up till now, though
a turning point in her life. She had always mana
ocked public opinion, she had always
herself outside the pale of society. The c
ike of Devonshire, the wife of William
ed to get away with a great deal that
d a less glorious personage.
private. But now she had given
s of actual violence, too, had always
she had also published her in
n a way that not even Lady O
l though the influence of her
g made an open outcast,
marked woman.

175

fell the br
leep, she w
e to Dublin
ion, swearin
ain. Howe
intimacy of
s her condi
selfish tend
devoted him
t brought te
ing to Dubl
aybreak thr

ady Bessbor
"When the
ked of how
him in fron
l vehemenc
r torturing,
she scream
the househo
Irish jig wi
ng outrageo

The Artist & Her Techniques

"Good fortune to you. Mine was a beautiful life."

—Sandra Evertson

Paris Flea Market Designs

An artist's relationship with her work is very personal. Often, she doesn't know what inspires her or how she comes up with her designs. She only knows that this is how she expresses herself, and to live any other way would be unthinkable.

While many share their muses, few share their methods. Lucky for us, Sandra Evertson is the exception. She is enthusiastic about teaching others to do what comes naturally to her.

Sandra grew up in a very creative family, joining her mother and grandmother on frequent trips to antique stores, thrift shops, and just about any other venue that yielded old things that seemed to tell a story. The winning find could be an old apron, or an everyday item made into something completely different.

Somewhere along the way Sandra developed an eye for interesting lettering and thus ignited her collection of out-of-print newspapers, books, and magazines and birth and marriage certificates. Once, she picked up a circa 1920 high school diploma just for the two inches of beautiful scroll at the bottom.

She also began to amass old photographs, particularly ones from the Victorian era with expressive eyes—joyful, mischievous, and ecstatic despite a somber face. As long as the eyes were revealing, they served as fodder for the artist.

Sandra dabbled in different mediums—from painting and drawing to making porcelain dolls and welding flowers. She opened a small antiques shop, where she bought and sold a bit of everything.

At work she dealt in vintage furnishings and accessories and at home she worked on paper collages. When she ran out of room, she started selling these one-of a-kinds in her shop. They always sold right away, and it wasn't long before her shop was filled with paper ballerinas and shadow boxes reminiscent of Moulin Rouge characters, costumes, and eclectic chaos.

Her paper designs are Baroque in feel, and the artist quickly admits to a penchant for turn-of-the-century European designs. She loves the ballet and has yet to give up collecting scraps of anything reminiscent of pre-1930s.

Today, Sandra's home is filled with containers of silver pots, wooden shoe forms, porcelain dolls, buttons, rhinestones, ribbons, beads, marbles, feathers, and so many other whimsical things. She has no shortage of ideas, and her creativity provides the inspirational backdrop to fashioning your own one-of-a-kinds.

123

ACKNOWLEDGEMENTS

Austin Antique Mall
Austin, Texas

Cala Antiques
San Luis Obispo, California
www.calaantiques.com

Cleaveland Antiques
Aurora, New York

Cupidz Clozet
Austin, Texas
www.cupidzclozet.com

Hillcrest Antiques
New Braunfels, Texas

Hobby Lobby
www.hobbylobby.com

Inspire Company
www.inspirecompany.com

Magnolia Pearl
Bandera, Texas
www.magnoliapearl.com

Michael's Art Supplies
www.michaels.com

New Bohemia
Austin, Texas

Paris Flea Market Designs
Gallery of artwork
www.parisfleamarketdesigns.com

Plaid Enterprises
www.plaidonline.com

ShabbyTiques.com
For Paris Flea Market Designs
Originals by Sandra Evertson
www.shabbytiques.com

Uncommon Objects
Austin, Texas

Photography by:
Ryan Hazen
Thomas McConnell

INDEX

Acknowledgments 124

Acrobats 44

Adhesives 10

Advertisements 100, 110

Antique books 24

Babbit's Cabbage 92

Ballet 28

Brass buttons 58

Breath freshener tin 16

Business cards 70, 76

Calling cards 70

Chandelier 32

Circle faces 11

Class clown 52

Cosmetic advertisement 100

Crepe paper 11, 16, 92

Cupcake Papier Mâché Box 38

Embellishments 10, 11

Flora Fairies—Lolly 70

German almanac 84

Gibberish Bandbox 118

Handkerchief 118

Higgins Playing Card Art Doll . . 58

High school diploma 52

Hole punch 11

Hot glue 11

Ladies Home Journal 110

Mail-order catalog 104

Milles Bons Baisers 62

Mint Julep 44

Mother Nature 20

Paint items 10

Paint pen 12

Paper effects 12

Paper elements 12

Paper Maker's Heart Bandbox . . . 24

Paper stars 44

Papier mâché 38

Paris Flea Market Designs 123

Petite Theatre 84

Petunia Art Doll 20

Pierrot 32

Pipsqueak 110

Playing cards 58

Posies 100

Postcard 62

Prima Ballerina 28

Sources 13

Spodie Odie Doll 52

Tarts Business Card Art Dolls . . . 76

Tempus Fugit 104

Theatre La Rousse 32

Tin container 16

Tips & Tricks of the Trade 11

Tools 10

Violet and Friends 16

METRIC EQUIVALENCY CHARTS

inches to millimeters and centimeters								yards to meters										
inches	mm	cm	inches	cm	inches	cm	yards	meters	yards	meters	yards	meters	yards	meters	yards	meters
⅛	3	0.3	9	22.9	30	76.2	⅛	0.11	2⅛	1.94	4⅛	3.77	6⅛	5.60	8⅛	7.43
¼	6	0.6	10	25.4	31	78.7	⅛	0.11	2⅛	1.94	4⅛	3.77	6⅛	5.60	8⅛	7.43
½	13	1.3	12	30.5	33	83.8	¼	0.23	2¼	2.06	4¼	3.89	6¼	5.72	8¼	7.54
⅜	16	1.6	13	33.0	34	86.4	⅜	0.34	2⅜	2.17	4⅜	4.00	6⅜	5.83	8⅜	7.66
¾	19	1.9	14	35.6	35	88.9	⅝	0.46	2½	2.29	4½	4.11	6½	5.94	8½	7.77
⅞	22	2.2	15	38.1	36	91.4	⅝	0.57	2⅝	2.40	4⅝	4.23	6⅝	6.06	8⅝	7.89
1	25	2.5	16	40.6	37	94.0	¾	0.69	2¾	2.51	4¾	4.34	6¾	6.17	8¾	8.00
1¼	32	3.2	17	43.2	38	96.5	⅞	0.80	2⅞	2.63	4⅞	4.46	6⅞	6.29	8⅞	8.12
1½	38	3.8	18	45.7	39	99.1	1	0.91	3	2.74	5	4.57	7	6.40	9	8.23
1¾	44	4.4	19	48.3	40	101.6	1¼	1.03	3¼	2.86	5⅛	4.69	7¼	6.52	9⅛	8.34
2	51	5.1	20	50.8	41	104.1	1¼	1.14	3¼	2.97	5¼	4.80	7¼	6.63	9¼	8.46
2½	64	6.4	21	53.3	42	106.7	1⅜	1.26	3⅜	3.09	5⅜	4.91	7⅜	6.74	9⅜	8.57
3	76	7.6	22	55.9	43	109.2	1½	1.37	3½	3.20	5½	5.03	7½	6.86	9½	8.69
3½	89	8.9	23	58.4	44	111.8	1⅝	1.49	3⅝	3.31	5⅝	5.14	7⅝	6.97	9⅝	8.80
4	102	10.2	24	61.0	45	114.3	1¾	1.60	3¾	3.43	5¾	5.26	7¾	7.09	9¾	8.92
4½	114	11.4	25	63.5	46	116.8	1⅞	1.71	3⅞	3.54	5⅞	5.37	7⅞	7.20	9⅞	9.03
5	127	12.7	26	66.0	47	119.4	2	1.83	4	3.66	6	5.49	8	7.32	10	9.14
6	152	15.2	27	68.6	48	121.9										
7	178	17.8	28	71.1	49	124.5										
8	203	20.3	29	73.7	50	127.0										

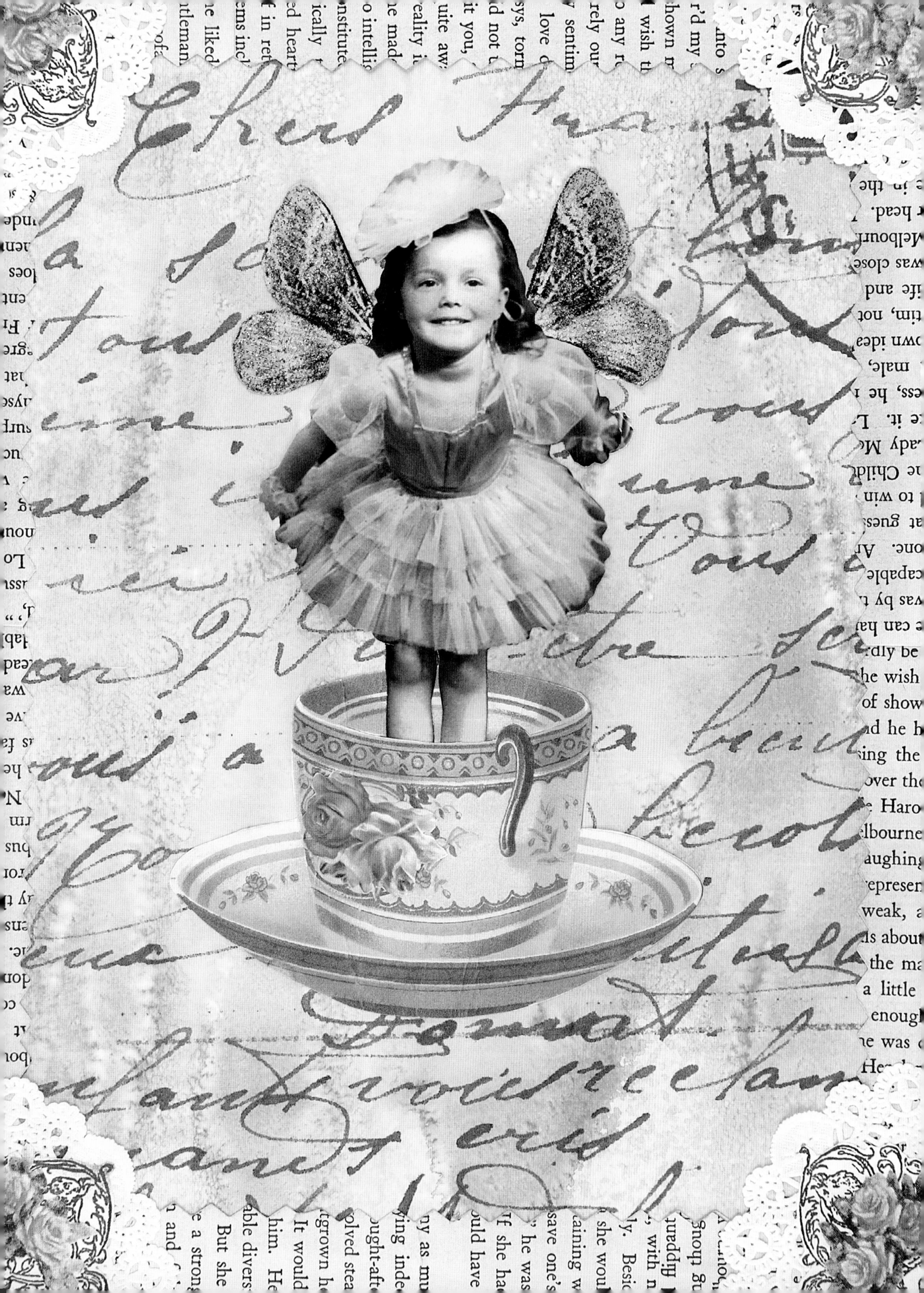